Better Learning Research Review

Niall Curry
Dadan
Allen Davenport
Maya Defianty
Linda Fisher
Karen Forbes
Christina Gkonou

Ben Knight
Judit Kormos
Betsy Parrish
Hayo Reinders
Silvana Richardson
Graham Skerritt
Kate Wilson

Peter Watkins

Shaftesbury Road, Cambridge CB2 8EA, United Kingdom

One Liberty Plaza, 20th Floor, New York, NY 10006, USA

477 Williamstown Road, Port Melbourne, VIC 3207, Australia

314–321, 3rd Floor, Plot 3, Splendor Forum, Jasola District Centre, New Delhi – 110025, India

103 Penang Road, #05-06/07, Visioncrest Commercial, Singapore 238467

Cambridge University Press & Assessment is a department of the University of Cambridge.

We share the University's mission to contribute to society through the pursuit of education, learning and research at the highest international levels of excellence.

www.cambridge.org
Information on this title: www.cambridge.org/9781009152150

© Cambridge University Press & Assessment 2022

This publication is in copyright. Subject to statutory exception and to the provisions of relevant collective licensing agreements, no reproduction of any part may take place without the written permission of Cambridge University Press & Assessment.

First published 2022

20 19 18 17 16 15 14 13 12 11 10 9 8 7 6 5 4 3 2

Printed in Great Britain by Ashford Colour Press Ltd.

A catalogue record for this publication is available from the British Library

ISBN   978-1-009-15215-0 Paperback
ISBN   978-1-009-15216-7 Cambridge Core eBook
ISBN   978-1-009-15214-3 eBook

Cambridge University Press & Assessment has no responsibility for the persistence or accuracy of URLs for external or third-party internet websites referred to in this publication, and does not guarantee that any content on such websites is, or will remain, accurate or appropriate.

Contents

Acknowledgements ... v

Introduction ... 1

Section 1: Teacher development and wellbeing

1 Christina Gkonou: Teacher wellbeing ... 7
2 Silvana Richardson: Building supportive teacher learning communities ... 13
3 Ben Knight: A research-based approach to professional development for English as a Medium of Learning teaching staff ... 21
4 Graham Skerritt: Evaluating the effectiveness of a teacher training programme ... 29

Section 2: Inclusivity, differentiation and learning strategies

5 Betsy Parrish: Differentiation by design – optimising learning in the English language classroom ... 47
6 Judit Kormos: Specific learning difficulties and inclusive language teaching material design ... 61
7 Karen Forbes: Language learning strategies ... 65

Section 3: Beyond language skills – creativity and critical thinking

8 Kate Wilson, Maya Defianty and Dadan: Critical thinking in the pandemic – the case of an Indonesian EFL classroom going online ... 71
9 Linda Fisher: Creating classroom conditions for creativity ... 79
10 Allen Davenport: Developing creativity in the ELT classroom ... 83

Section 4: Data and technology

11 Hayo Reinders: Making sense of big (and not so big) data with language learning analytics ... 91
12 Niall Curry: Digital pedagogy and language teaching and learning – from research to practice ... 103

About the authors ... 111

Acknowledgements

The authors and publishers acknowledge the following sources of copyright material and are grateful for the permissions granted. While every effort has been made, it has not always been possible to identify the sources of all the material used, or to trace all copyright holders. If any omissions are brought to our notice, we will be happy to include the appropriate acknowledgements on reprinting and in the next update to the digital edition, as applicable.

Keys: C = Chapter

Text

C7: Multilingual Matters for the figure taken from *Cross-Linguistic Transfer of Writing Strategies: Interactions Between Foreign Language and First Language Classrooms* by Karen Forbes. Copyright © 2020 Multilingual Matters. Reproduced with permission; C10: Kyung Hee Kim for the adapted text taken from 'The Torrance tests of creative thinking – figural or verbal: Which one should we use?' by Kyung Hee Kim. Copyright © 2017 Kyung Hee Kim. Reproduced with kind permission.

Photos

C5: Reproduced with kind permission of Sina Taghavi, Remy Taghavi and Betsy Parrish; C11: Euan Bonner and Hayo Reinders for the screengrab taken from https://www.classmoto.com/. Classmoto © 2022 Chihippo Creations. Reprinted with kind permission of Euan Bonner and Hayo Reinders.

Cover photography by alvarez/E+/Getty Images.

Typeset

Typesetting by Blooberry Design Ltd.

URLS

The publisher has used its best endeavours to ensure that the URLs for external websites referred to in this book are correct and active at the time of going to press. However, the publisher has no responsibility for the websites and can make no guarantee that a site will remain live or that the content is or will remain appropriate.

Introduction
Peter Watkins

As the title suggests, this book is a review of the research in which Cambridge University Press has recently been involved. It is a celebration of both the specific outcomes of that research and, just as importantly, of the collaborations that are built when researchers, teachers and institutions work together to gain insight into issues of mutual interest.

For many teachers, the word 'research' has connotations of the positivist tradition associated with the hard sciences – control groups, pre- and post-tests and large-scale quantitative data – leading to results that the researchers can reasonably claim to be generalisable. While such research is no doubt valuable, it is only one view of research. Research can also move away from the experimental designs that these notions imply and instead adopt a small-scale and local perspective, which might address immediate classroom concerns, making use of largely qualitative data. Whereas teachers may feel that they could never reasonably conduct a large-scale study due to constraints of time, they may see opportunities to conduct small-scale research reflecting on their own teaching and learning contexts and their own practice. This can be empowering as it gives teachers the opportunity to create knowledge which is immediately relevant to them, as well as consume the knowledge generated by others. Even where teachers are not directly involved in conducting the research themselves, they may identify with the practical focus that small-scale research projects often have.

Teachers, and others, can also make a contribution to our shared knowledge when they take the research conducted by others, analyse it, and then apply it to new situations. For example, research from cognitive psychology tells us how people are likely to remember new information and we can build on that, and make a further contribution to knowledge, by transforming these insights into practical classroom activities that teachers can make use of in their professional lives. In other words, we examine the existing research evidence and see the implications that it has for classroom practice.

For the purposes of this book, we see value in all such activities, from the large scale to that focused on a particular context, and from generating primary (original) data to that which seeks to interpret and reapply the work of others to new contexts.

Who is this book for?

This book is for anyone who is interested in language teaching. Obviously, that includes teachers and we hope that some of the articles here give ideas for evidence-informed activities that can be used directly in the classroom. However, as well as serving that practical purpose, we hope the articles will promote reflection on broader issues that rightly concern teachers – from their own wellbeing to ensuring that they have an inclusive classroom and much more besides.

The book is not solely for teachers. We hope that teacher educators and others who are responsible for providing professional development for colleagues will also find the book useful. For example, relevant articles can be selected and might be used as a basis for group discussions. Furthermore, the articles here might prompt ideas for teacher action research projects that focus on the immediate concerns of teachers in a particular context.

As well as teachers and teacher educators, we also hope that administrators and managers will find some of these articles of use, as they plan, implement and evaluate interventions designed to create better learning for the students they serve.

How the book is organised

In order to keep the book accessible, none of the articles included here could be considered particularly long by academic standards and some are very short. Given the busy professional lives of teachers, we hope that this facilitates readers being able to engage with the articles even if they have only a few minutes to spare at any particular time.

In order to promote reflection, all but the shortest of the articles include questions at the end to stimulate the reflection process. These can, of course, be considered by individuals as they read but may also initiate group discussions among teachers if the articles are used to prompt wider discussions of issues that affect teachers' professional lives. The questions are not intended to check understanding or to limit thought, but instead they are designed to prompt initial ideas that can then be developed in the light of the evidence provided.

The articles are divided into four broad themes. The first section is titled *Teacher development and wellbeing* and, as the name suggests, deals with issues directly concerning teachers. Christina Gkonou discusses teacher wellbeing and, in particular, its implications for classroom practice and teacher education. Silvana Richardson looks at ways in which professional development can be efficiently supported through the building of teacher learning communities. Ben Knight considers the needs of teachers working in institutions where English is the medium of instruction. In the final paper of the section, Graham Skerritt evaluates a teacher development programme in Japan in which Cambridge University Press worked with the Japanese Ministry of Education, Culture, Sports, Science and Technology.

Section 2 moves on to look at issues concerning our learners and is titled *Inclusivity, differentiation and learning strategies*. Betsy Parrish shows us how we can make differentiation work in our classrooms, sometimes with quite small adjustments to our existing practice. Judit Kormos discusses how we can design material that is more inclusive by catering for the needs of learners who have specific learning difficulties, and Karen Forbes looks at how we can teach language learning strategies in the classroom.

In Section 3, *Beyond language skills – creativity and critical thinking*, we look at what are sometimes referred to as '21st-century skills'. Specifically, there are papers on fostering creativity and critical thinking. Kate Wilson, Maya Defianty and Dadan report on a 2020 research project, in which Indonesian EFL teachers described how they support their learners in critical thinking, and this paper focuses particularly on the innovative approaches adopted by one of those teachers. Linda Fisher and Allen Davenport both consider creativity, discussing respectively the conditions necessary for creativity and how creativity can be developed in the classroom.

The last section of the book is called *Data and technology*, and includes an article by Hayo Reinders on the pedagogical applications of 'big data'. We conclude with an article by Niall Curry, who considers the research into digital pedagogy and its implications for practice.

Whatever your role is in language teaching, we hope that you find the research reported in this book stimulating and that the articles prove to be both useful and enjoyable.

Section 1: Teacher development and wellbeing

1 Teacher wellbeing
Christina Gkonou

Introduction

Teachers constitute an important part – if not the most important – of the school workforce, and their everyday classroom practice is often influenced by their own psychologies and emotions. If teachers are well, they will also teach well (Holmes, 2005). High levels of teacher wellbeing can increase the effectiveness of teaching as well as the quality of student learning. In other words, teacher wellbeing does not just impact positively upon teachers but also upon learners.

Since March 2020, the world of education has been severely afflicted by the outbreak of the global pandemic of Covid-19, with teacher (and student) wellbeing suffering considerably and levels of teacher (and student) stress rising dramatically. Thus, attending to teacher wellbeing has now become more topical than ever before.

In this article, I start by explaining what wellbeing is and why teacher wellbeing matters. I then discuss some of the implications of what we already know about teacher wellbeing for classroom practice and for language teacher education, highlighting the necessity for the latter to incorporate wellbeing into its pre-service and in-service programmes and curricula. Throughout the article, I summarise findings of the as yet scant research into language teacher wellbeing and emotions, and what lessons we can draw from it.

What is wellbeing?

Wellbeing is often seen as the opposite of stress and a state in which individuals are feeling good and functioning well. Although this conceptualisation of wellbeing is to some extent true, wellbeing is a lot more than that. First, wellbeing is associated with stress and, in fact, in trying to nourish and increase our wellbeing we would in the first place need to manage our stress. However, it is worth clarifying that wellbeing and stress are not exact opposites; if we do not feel stressed, this does not necessarily mean that we are experiencing high levels of wellbeing. Second, although wellbeing is a positively toned word and concept, it does not just refer to how we can be relaxed and happy all the time (Holmes, 2019). More often than not, positive wellbeing comes after times of crisis and hardship – and individuals' continuous efforts to overcome such challenging moments. In our collaborative work with Elizabeth R. Miller since 2016, we have focused on experienced English language teachers' emotions and subsequent emotion regulation practices as narrated in interview accounts. We found that teachers experience emotional rewards after going through significant emotional turmoil and critical incidents, which have had a long-lasting influence on their psychology, teacher identity and teaching practice (Miller and Gkonou, 2018; Gkonou and Miller, 2020). Albeit difficult to handle, these emotional challenges helped teachers to gain emotional capital; in other words, teachers learned how to manage their emotions and improve their wellbeing as a result of undergoing such challenges (Gkonou and Miller, 2021).

Additionally, although many of us would link wellbeing with mental health and thus with its emotional dimension, other types of wellbeing are equally important. Think, for instance, of our physical wellbeing and physical health and how important it is to do some exercise as often as we can, even if this is just going out for a walk. Intellectual and spiritual wellbeing also have a role to play in our behaviour, performance and psychology. These refer, for example, to staying connected with arts and literature, and finding meaning and purpose in life. All of these types of wellbeing create a wellbeing system or network, and if one part of this network fails, then the entire wellbeing system is likely to collapse too.

Why does teacher wellbeing matter?

It is widely known that teachers lead busy lives (Day and Gu, 2010) and that teaching is often listed among the most stressful professions (Lovewell, 2012). This is because of multiple professional commitments and a number of challenges in the workplace, such as lack of support, disengaged students, interpersonal relationships that need to be handled with care, lack of autonomy, low salaries and often precarious contracts, and excessive workloads, with work often being continued at home (MacIntyre et al., 2019; Mercer and Gregersen, 2020). Coupled with additional stressors in response to Covid-19, such as mandatory work-from-home policies, work-life imbalance and work-life spillover, social distancing rules, technology failures and a sudden switch to online teaching with little – if any at all – prior training, the profession has become ever more stressful (MacIntyre et al., 2020). Juggling personal and professional roles and trying to manage the above challenges poses a direct threat to teacher wellbeing, thus making it vitally important for teachers to attend to their wellbeing and practise self-care through adopting appropriate coping mechanisms.

One reason, therefore, why teacher wellbeing matters is connected with the need to manage stressors in the workplace, with a view to improving performance and the quality of teaching. Another reason concerns the process of psychological or emotional contagion, where teacher emotions and wellbeing influence student emotions and wellbeing (Frenzel and

Stephens, 2013). When such contagion happens, it can also affect student success – positively if the emotions transferred from teachers to students are conducive to learning, and negatively if teachers experience a lot of stress and their emotions are unpleasant and difficult. Students can pick up on this and get stressed too.

What also makes teacher wellbeing key in education is the fact that all teachers are likely to be affected by low levels of wellbeing. This is in contrast with common misconceptions that it is mainly the newly qualified teachers who cannot cope and, therefore, usually leave the profession within the first five years of training (Guarino et al., 2006). Although teacher attrition is particularly common among early-career teachers (UNESCO Institute for Statistics, 2016), mid-career teachers and highly experienced teachers (who might also be in managerial posts) are likely to be affected by low wellbeing too, for different reasons: the former because they might have been going through prolonged periods of stress and the latter because they need to attend to their own wellbeing as well as the wellbeing of the teachers that they manage. In our book for Cambridge University Press on cultivating teacher wellbeing (Brierton and Gkonou, 2022), we present vignettes and stories of teachers at different career stages, roles and educational settings to demonstrate that wellbeing can be a concern for any teacher, irrespective of their stage of career. This makes wellbeing an essential component for all teachers and strategies for supporting wellbeing an integral part of classroom practice and teacher education.

Implications for classroom practice

In class, teacher wellbeing could be promoted through healthy interpersonal relationships, mainly between the teacher and students but also amongst students. Teacher-student relationships should ideally share the following relationship qualities: honesty, trust, respect and responsiveness (Gkonou and Mercer, 2017; Mercer and Gkonou, 2020). Empathy should also be added to the list, as it caters for relational depth, skills in being a careful listener, and effective communication and understanding among classroom members. It is important for teachers and students to be able to understand when a classroom relationship is difficult and not working well. It is also equally important for teachers to appreciate classroom diversity and to be fair and consistent with all students. All of these qualities, which are also key socio-emotional competencies to be fostered in contemporary classrooms, can help towards improving teacher and student wellbeing and, subsequently, the conditions for classroom learning and teaching.

Healthy teacher-student relationships also help teachers to understand and explain possible instances of student misconduct, which is often cited as a source of teacher stress (Kyriacou, 2001; Rogers, 2012). Teachers' beliefs about student misbehaviour are often negative, as teachers tend to think that a student misbehaves because they resent the teacher. Through such limiting beliefs, teachers then question their teaching abilities and self-worth, which decreases their confidence and wellbeing. However, when students misbehave, it is usually due to reasons that extend beyond the language class and have barely anything to do with the teacher. Knowing how to investigate student misbehaviour and what action to take is a key step towards safeguarding both teacher and student wellbeing inside the classroom.

Any strategies for supporting wellbeing inside the classroom are unlikely to have any lasting value if teachers are not supported in this journey by other members of the school community and, above all, by their educational managers, who lay the foundations for how their school operates. Therefore, a whole-school approach to wellbeing and possibly also a whole-school cultural change with respect to wellbeing are needed. This would mean that the whole school (including senior school leadership, teachers, students, parents and support staff) is attuned to the fundamental role of wellbeing in better learning and teaching and takes action to address it in school practice.

Implications for teacher education

Teacher education could and should do better in supporting and promoting teacher wellbeing, especially in the current post-pandemic period. Although discussions on wellbeing within education are taking place through webinars and talks, teachers would benefit from explicit, focused training on different aspects of wellbeing and concrete ideas about how their wellbeing could be nourished. Such training should be incorporated into both pre-service and in-service teacher education programmes to meet the needs of teachers of all career stages.

To inform training and what it should cover with respect to wellbeing, more research is needed, as it would help to try out possible interventions for wellbeing and test their effectiveness for classroom practice prior to adding them to teacher training programmes. In Brierton and Gkonou (2022), we have produced a lengthy training toolkit, with three workshops targeting different aspects of wellbeing. Each workshop includes five one-hour sessions with practical activities. We have already had the opportunity to pilot several of these activities with teachers – a vital first step in developing an evidence-based wellbeing component within broader teacher education programmes. The workshops focus on the following areas:

- Understanding the mind, how emotion regulation could be practised and how psychological safety could be established in class.
- Cultivating teachers' own wellbeing through increasing emotional self-awareness, understanding self-criticism, accepting emotions, developing self-compassion and setting healthy work-life boundaries.
- Addressing wellbeing inside the classroom through understanding the qualities of a positive relationship, building strong teacher-student relationships, becoming resilient and developing a growth mindset, and promoting effective group work in class.

This is a first attempt towards producing full training days on the topic of teacher wellbeing for use with language teachers and educational managers. It is both the groundwork and a call for more work (through research and pilot programmes) towards updating teachers' skills related to wellbeing, and officially introducing wellbeing in formal, well-recognised teacher education programmes which also lead to certification and teaching qualifications.

Reflection

1. In your career, what things have been the principal stressors with which you have had to deal?
2. What particular events in your career have most boosted your wellbeing?
3. Look at the bullet point list above of possible areas that teacher education workshops on wellbeing might cover. Which areas do you think would most benefit you and your colleagues?
4. Are there any interventions aimed at supporting teacher wellbeing that could be put into place quickly in your context?

References

Brierton, K., & Gkonou, C. (2022). *Cultivating Teacher Wellbeing*. Cambridge: Cambridge University Press.

Day, C., & Gu, Q. (2010). *The New Lives of Teachers*. Abingdon: Routledge.

Frenzel, A. C., & Stephens, E. J. (2013). Emotions. In N. C. Hall & T. Goetz (eds.), *Emotion, Motivation, and Self-Regulation: A Handbook for Teachers* (1–56). Bingley: Emerald Group Publishing Limited.

Gkonou, C., & Mercer, S. (2017). *Understanding Emotional and Social Intelligence Among English Language Teachers*. London: British Council.

Gkonou, C., & Miller, E. R. (2020). Critical incidents in language teachers' narratives of emotional experience. In C. Gkonou, J.-M. Dewaele & J. King (eds.), *The Emotional Rollercoaster of Language Teaching* (131–149). Bristol: Multilingual Matters.

Gkonou, C., & Miller, E. R. (2021). An exploration of language teacher reflection, emotion labor, and emotional capital. *TESOL Quarterly*, 55(1), 134–155.

Guarino, C. M., Santibañez, L., & Daley, G. A. (2006). Teacher recruitment and retention: A review of the recent empirical literature. *Review of Educational Research*, 76(2), 173–208.

Holmes, E. (2005). *Teacher Wellbeing: Looking After Yourself and Your Career in the Classroom*. Abingdon: Routledge.

Holmes, E. (2019). *A Practical Guide to Teacher Wellbeing*. London: Sage.

Kyriacou, C. (2001). Teacher stress: Directions for further research. *Educational Review*, 53(1), 27–35. https://doi.org/10.1080/00131910120033628

Lovewell, K. (2012). *Every Teacher Matters: Inspiring Well-being Through Mindfulness*. St Albans, Herts: Ecademy Press.

MacIntyre, P. D., Gregersen, T., & Mercer, S. (2020). Language teachers' coping strategies during the Covid-19 conversion to online teaching: Correlations with stress, wellbeing and negative emotions. *System*, 94, 102352.

MacIntyre, P. D., Ross, J., Talbot, K., Mercer, S., Gregersen, T., & Banga, C. A. (2019). Stressors, personality and wellbeing among language teachers. *System*, 82, 26–38.

Mercer, S., & Gkonou, C. (2020). Relationships and good language teachers. In C. Griffiths & Z. Tajeddin (eds.), *Lessons From Good Language Teachers* (164–174). Cambridge: Cambridge University Press.

Mercer, S., & Gregersen, T. (2020). *Teacher Wellbeing*. Oxford: Oxford University Press.

Miller, E. R., & Gkonou, C. (2018). Language teacher agency, emotion labor and emotional rewards in tertiary-level English language programs. *System*, 79, 49–59. https://doi.org/10.1016/j.system.2018.03.002

Rogers, B. (2012). *The Essential Guide to Managing Teacher Stress: Practical Skills for Teachers*. Harlow: Pearson Education Limited.

UNESCO Institute for Statistics (2016). *The World Needs Almost 69 Million New Teachers to Reach the 2030 Education Goals*. Available at: http://uis.unesco.org/en/files/fs39-world-needs-almost-69-million-new-teachers-reach-2030-education-goals-2016-en-pdf

2 Building supportive teacher learning communities
Silvana Richardson

Introduction

It is widely acknowledged that teacher learning which is undertaken as a collaborative endeavour within a supportive environment can be an invaluable tool for professional development. Research published before the Covid-19 pandemic found that teachers working in more supportive professional environments become more effective over time than those working in less supportive contexts (Kraft and Papay, 2014); in addition, effective peer collaboration among teachers – i.e. working together to solve problems, and trying out and refining new approaches focused on achieving better learning for students – can lead to deep and transferable teacher learning, with potential for impact on student learning (Cordingley et al., 2015).

Since early 2020, however, the massive disruption caused by the pandemic has adversely affected organisation-driven teacher learning in many organisations. Shrinking academic teams, cuts to continuing professional development (CPD) budgets and a marked increase in teachers' workloads made it extremely challenging to offer any kind of sustained CPD provision. Unfortunately, such unfavourable conditions for collective teacher learning unfolded just when many teachers were most in need of support, as they attempted to learn new skills quickly.

As the education sector begins to transition out of the pandemic, the extent of lost learning highlights the urgent need for students to be supported so that those losses can be made up. In this context, two facts become self-evident: (1) that teachers play a central role as key enablers of student learning and recovery; and (2) that most teachers – the main drivers of the recovery phase – are already exhausted and running on depleted funds of resilience and adaptability. Therefore, supporting teachers and their learning (during and beyond the transition), by bringing them together to learn in supportive learning communities, should be a priority for every education provider in the short and medium terms. Given current constraints, this prioritisation needs to take account of the need to find affordable and resourceful solutions for professional learning, to ensure that CPD remains viable and sustainable.

Why supportive teacher learning communities?

In contrast to other spontaneous or 'engineered' supportive spaces for teachers to gather together (e.g. the virtual end of the week meet-up), teacher learning communities focus on a common goal that really matters to those teachers: transferable learning – i.e. professional learning which they can enact in their teaching. A focus on agile transferable learning will continue to be crucial during the recovery phase, due to the scale of change to be expected in language teaching organisations (LTOs): namely, the shift from an unplanned and rapid move to online learning to a strategic and managed growth of online education, and the implementation of cost-effective but logistically and pedagogically complex approaches to teaching and learning. For example, added to the complexity and relative newness of having to teach in socially-distanced and hybrid physical and virtual environments, teachers are also finding themselves teaching increasingly disparate mixed-level classes, particularly in the private sub-sector, which has been worst hit, both economically and in terms of student recruitment.

In these circumstances, supportive teacher learning communities offer both a conducive environment for capacity building and a comforting sense that 'we are in this together' at the same time. As Doris Santoro remarks:

> 'Whenever teachers are brought in to investigate and develop interventions, you're creating opportunities for authentic community and taking action, in a way that feels less isolating.'
> (in Walker, 2018)

A practical framework for facilitating supportive teacher learning communities in difficult times

For many LTOs, this is not the time to implement prolonged, ambitious, costly and time-consuming approaches to teacher research, which often require buying in external expertise and paying for sustained teacher cover. However, a viable workaround is to consider the key features of impactful approaches to teacher research and to adapt them as focused, practical and immediately relevant experiences, which result in transferable learning for teachers.

The following suggestions offer a pragmatic approach to professional development in supportive teacher learning communities, which address three concerns at this critical time:

1. keeping organisation-driven teacher learning alive
2. supporting collective and collaborative teacher learning
3. putting in place viable and affordable CPD solutions.

The Six Ds Cycle

The Six Ds Cycle is a framework for facilitating scaffolded teacher experimentation and sharing with colleagues in synchronous online or face-to-face TeachMeets[1] and/or participation in asynchronous forums.

The aim of the cycle is for teachers to work together to find solutions to specific needs and briefly test whether they work. The nature of the cycle encourages teacher agency, supportive collaboration, transferability of hypotheseses to practice, evaluation, and sharing the resulting learning with colleagues. It is summarised in Figure 2.1 and explained in Table 2.1 below:

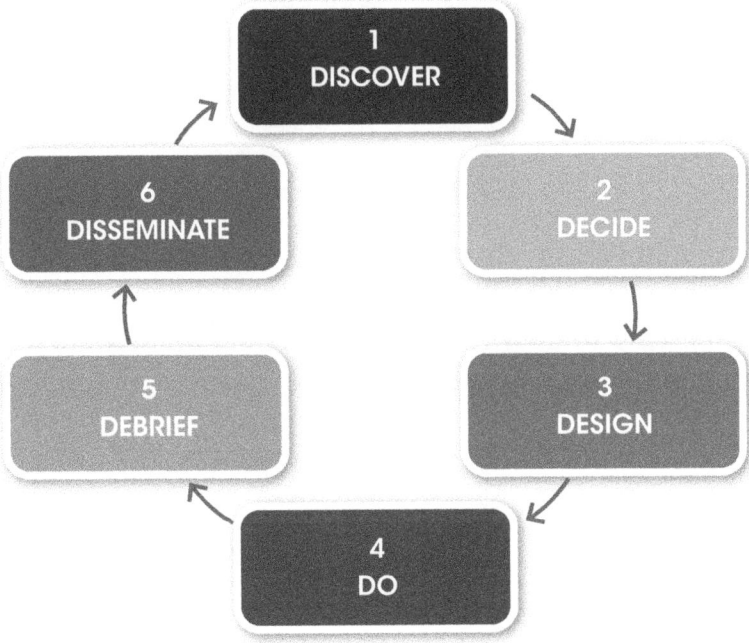

Figure 2.1: The Six Ds Cycle

---

[1] TeachMeets are organised, practical and informal meetings in which teachers share innovations and insights into their teaching practices.

Table 2.1: The Six Ds Cycle explained

STEP	PURPOSE	EXAMPLE	GUIDING QUESTIONS
1. DISCOVER	Teachers jointly consider possible solutions to a specific need	After having used breakout rooms for some time and noticing passive/limited student engagement during whole-class feedback following group work in breakout rooms, a group of teachers decide to explore what more they could do to maximise students' active and sustained engagement at that stage in synchronous online lessons. They brainstorm and discuss a number of alternatives.	What (else) could we try? What's out there that might be useful for us?
2. DECIDE	Teachers decide which of the solutions they looked into they will experiment with	The teachers decide to: a) get students to type joint notes during group work in breakout rooms, and copy/paste their notes onto a shared whole-class whiteboard b) ask students to react to other groups' notes, using annotations and reactions (e.g. type a question or comment, insert a tick/cross for agreement/disagreement, heart for 'I love that idea', question mark for 'I'm not sure what you mean,' etc.) c) use the students' annotations and reactions to inform the ensuing discussion, e.g. 'pouncing and bouncing'[2] accordingly.	What are we going to try?

---

2 'Pounce and Bounce' is a nomination strategy used during whole-class feedback to ensure that students' engagement is sustained throughout. It consists of nominating a student to participate (POUNCE) and then nominating other students to react, expand and challenge what was said previously by the other learner(s) (BOUNCE).

STEP	PURPOSE	EXAMPLE	GUIDING QUESTIONS
3. DESIGN	Teachers plan a short and simple experiment to try out the chosen strategy and then evaluate it	The teachers decide to: a) experiment with the procedure with their classes for a week, during feedback on 'meaty' tasks (communicative activities that elicit an extended answer) b) record three lessons: one at the end of the previous week without using the procedure, one in the middle and another one at the end of the week using it c) watch the videos to compare the nature of students' engagement during the feedback stages in the three lessons.	Who are we going to try this out with? (i.e. with which classes?) When are we going to try it? For how long? How are we going to implement it? How are we going to know whether it works?
4. DO	Teachers experiment with the new strategy	The teachers implement the procedure and record the three lessons using a video meeting platform, such as Zoom.	What do I need to do? In what sequence? What materials and resources do I need?
5. DEBRIEF	Teachers evaluate the experiment: whether it led to better learning; what 'tweaks' could improve it; whether other colleagues might benefit from trying it out	Each teacher watches the feedback stages on meaty tasks in their three recorded lessons and notices what happens. They take notes under two headings: 'What went well…' and 'Even better if….'. They then discuss their discoveries and thoughts, and decide whether to present these to other colleagues.	How well did it work? Is it worth developing further? If it is, then what changes could we make next time? Is it worth sharing what we have learnt with our colleagues?
6. DISSEMINATE	Teachers 'show and tell' their colleagues about their experiment, discoveries and take-aways	The teachers share their findings using the 'Off-The-Peg' Show and Tell frame (see below).	What do our colleagues need to know to understand our experiment and what we have learnt from it? What examples (samples of students' work, etc.) could we use to illustrate our points clearly? How could we structure and sequence our 'show and tell' so it is brief, focused, practical and useful to our colleagues?

Peer support and collaboration can be built throughout. For example, steps 1, 2, 3, 5 and 6 could take place as short and focused synchronous (face-to-face or online) CPD meetings with group feedback, or asynchronously through forums or through creating an online chat group for the teachers in the community.

Off-The-Peg Show and Tell

'Show and Tell' is a well-known procedure for teachers to share a practice they have implemented with their colleagues. It consists of demonstrating that practice, and/or showing relevant resources to illustrate it, such as a video excerpt, or materials produced by themselves or their students (SHOWING) and describing and explaining that practice (TELLING).

When effectively executed – i.e. when teachers share a practice that is new and relevant to all their colleagues and based on a solid rationale, and when the 'Show and Tell' is clearly structured and appropriately sequenced – it can inspire peers to experiment and expand their own pedagogic repertoire. That said, its aim is mainly to raise awareness, hopefully motivating colleagues to try it out in their own practice, which means that by itself it is unlikely to lead to transferable teacher learning. However, if integrated within The Six Ds Cycle – as a possible Step 6: DISSEMINATE – it can offer ideas for Step 1: DISCOVER of a new cycle.

The following 'Off-The-Peg' Show and Tell Frame can be used in different ways to ensure that 'Shows and Tells' remain focused and to the point, while including all the key elements needed for teachers to understand what the practice consists of, how it can be implemented, in which contexts and settings it can be enacted, and why it might be advantageous to use it.

'OFF-THE-PEG' SHOW AND TELL FRAME
I've tried.................... (NAME ACTIVITY / TECHNIQUE / ED TECHNOLOGY SOLUTION)
with my... (DESCRIBE CLASS)
because.. (STATE REASON FOR CHOICE).
This is how it works:....................................... (DESCRIBE AND SHOW PROCEDURE).
It worked.. (EVALUATE).
I recommend it because.. (REASON TO TRY IT).
Perhaps you might want to................ (SUGGESTION – e.g. FOR CLASS, VARIATION).

Figure 2.2: Example of an 'Off-The-Peg' Show and Tell Frame

Conclusion

Supportive teacher learning communities offer safe 'sandpits' for teachers to try out new approaches and can be powerhouses of creative strategies, practical solutions and increased teacher confidence. At the same time, they are places of connection and belonging where teachers can find inspiration and support in times of uncertainty and instability.

The strategies presented above provide a framework to sustain a supportive teacher learning community in difficult times. They address teachers' learning needs, are cost-effective, require low/no preparation from academic managers, and offer a scaffold for agile and collaborative experimentation.

Reflection

1. What types of CPD have you experienced in the past? Which have been most useful to you?
2. Look back at the first step (DISCOVER) in The Six Ds Cycle. In your teaching context, what would your priority for discovery be? How could you start your investigation?
3. How could you disseminate your findings in your institution? Might there be opportunities for wider dissemination?

References

Cordingley, P., Higgins, S., Greany, T., Buckler, N., Coles-Jordan, D., Crisp, B., Saunders, L., & Coe, R. (2015). *Developing Great Teaching: Lessons From the International Reviews Into Effective Professional Development*. Project Report. Teacher Development Trust, London. Available at: https://dro.dur.ac.uk/15834/1/15834.pdf?DDD45+DDD29+DDO128+hsmz78+d700tmt

Kraft, M. A., & Papay, J. P. (2014). Can professional environments in schools promote teacher development? Explaining heterogeneity in returns to teaching experience. *Educational Evaluation and Policy Analysis*, 36(4), 476–500. doi.org/10.3102/0162373713519496

Walker, T. (2018). *Teacher Burnout or Demoralization? What's the Difference and Why it Matters. NEA Today*. National Education Association. Available at: https://www.nea.org/advocating-for-change/new-from-nea/teacher-burnout-or-demoralization-whats-difference-and-why-it

3 A research-based approach to professional development for English as a Medium of Learning teaching staff
Ben Knight

Introduction

The trend towards increasingly teaching subject content through English, to students whose first language is not English, is well known (Galloway et al., 2020). The attractiveness of this approach from a political or managerial point of view is fairly obvious: students are learning both English and the subject at the same time – two for the price of one. But how effective is it? It is difficult to reach a clear conclusion on this as the contexts of its use are so varied (Galloway, 2017). However, one area that does come through clearly in the research is that it can only be effective if adequate training is provided for the teaching staff (Lee, 2010; Hadisantosa et al., 2010; Mehisto, 2012; Genesee and Hamayan, 2016; Thuy, 2016). For this reason, Cambridge University Press has been working on building up a better understanding of what the parameters are for effective professional development for these English medium programmes.

Scope and terminology

First, we need to clarify our scope and terminology. Programmes where English is the medium for learning will vary according to how much focus is given to the language learning part of it. In some cases, the focus is all on learning the curriculum subject, and no attention is given formally to the language learning dimension. In other cases, the focus is more on the language learning, with subject content being the application of the language learning. Figure 3.1 summarises the principal range of contexts in English as a Medium of Learning.

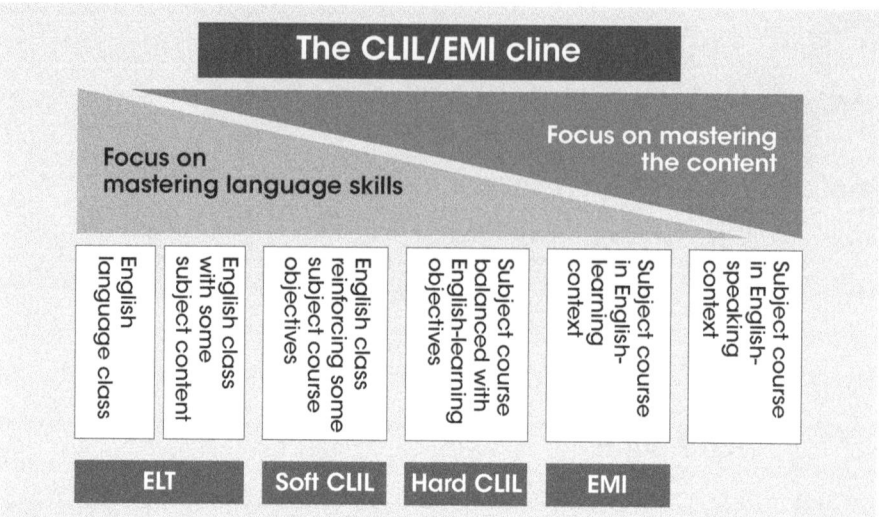

Figure 3.1: A summary of the principal range of contexts in EML

At Cambridge University Press, we use the term English as a Medium of Learning (EML) as an umbrella term for this range of CLIL/EMI contexts. The term 'bilingual' is also used in some contexts for programmes across this spectrum, from CLIL to EMI (Cambridge Assessment International Education, 2017).

Understanding the issues

As a first step, we carried out research into the main issues that EML teachers and co-ordinators face in running EML programmes. One input into this was a collaborative project with the University of Murcia, looking at the professional development needs of subject lecturers in an EML programme. While the lecturers recognised the language learning needs of their students, they generally lacked an understanding of how they could meet those needs. They often needed guidance on how their teaching might be adapted for the EML context and the options available to them for addressing language issues. They sometimes struggled to identify the precise linguistic needs of their students and what it was reasonable to expect from them.

In a survey of 33 institutions across 18 countries, we found the following results for the identification of problems teachers face with EML programmes. (In our survey we used the term EMI because we felt that this was the most easily recognised by the respondents and that it would be understood to cover the range of CLIL/EMI contexts described above.)

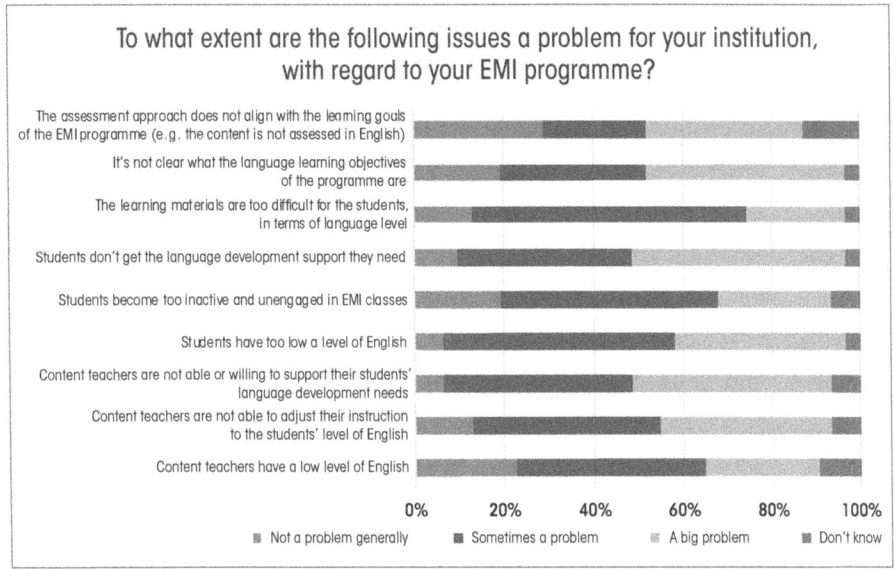

Figure 3.2: Survey results highlighting the issues teachers face when delivering EML programmes

The biggest problems identified by the teachers in this survey appeared to be related to support for their students' language development. Combining our research with other research on the challenges of EML programmes, such as Butler (2005), we grouped these into six main areas:

AREA	PRINCIPAL DIFFICULTIES OR CHALLENGES
Teachers/ Instructors	**Language proficiency:** subject teachers lack the language skills to explain concepts and information clearly. **Ability to support language needs:** subject teachers lack the ability to identify their students' language needs and help them deal with them. **Role:** subject teachers do not see it as part of their role to address language issues.
Learners	**Language proficiency:** students lack the language skills to follow the subject course in English (Yassin et al., 2009).
Curriculum	There is a lack of clarity about the objectives of the programme – for example, what the balance is between subject knowledge and language skills.
Pedagogy	Students can't follow the teacher. Students become passive. Students are not developing their English skills during the programme.
Resources	The resources/materials are designed for students who are very proficient in English (Lochmiller et al., 2016; Milligan et al., 2016).
Assessment	The assessment does not reflect the objectives of the programme – for example, the assessment of language skills needs to reflect the language learning objectives of the programme.

Table 3.1: The principal difficulties or challenges faced by teachers when delivering EML programmes

Addressing the issues

A number of these issues need to be addressed through the professional development of the teaching staff – both subject teachers and English language teachers.

From this, the key components of an effective Continuing Professional Development (CPD) programme were identified, with reference to other research on EML CPD programmes (Pavón Vázquez et al., 2015). These cover three main areas of development:

1. understanding the CLIL/EML approach of the institution
2. language skills / proficiency
3. EML pedagogy.

The exact balance of these components within a specific programme would obviously be determined by the precise needs of the participants. In the first area, a number of topics need to be covered:

- What are the objectives of the programme?
- How significant is successful language learning within the programme?
- What are the additional issues that L2 speakers of English face on an EML programme?
- What approach is there to use of the students' L1 and of translanguaging in the classroom?
- What role does the subject teacher play in students' language development?
- Will language skills be assessed directly or indirectly?
- In which ways should the language and subject teachers collaborate?
- Are language assistants to be used and, if so, how?

For teachers to be clear about these aspects of the programme, it is essential for the institution to be clear on these important questions. Therefore, the first step is establishing guidelines and policy for the institution's EML approach.

In the second area, language skills/proficiency, we need to distinguish between the different components of language skill (Evans, 2018). To some extent, the language of general English programmes – Basic Interpersonal Communication Skills (BICS) – is important, to build up an atmosphere of social contact and collaboration within the classroom. But there also needs to be a focus on two other key areas: Classroom Language and Cognitive Academic Language Proficiency (CALP).

Classroom Language covers the language needed to manage learning in a classroom ('work in pairs', 'let's check the homework', etc.), while CALP is the more academic language, and is generally divided into 'concept-rich' language and 'concept-supportive' language. Concept-rich language generally refers to vocabulary used to express concepts and information which form part of the subject curriculum, e.g. for plant science it would include vocabulary such as *photosynthesis* and *ecosystem*. Concept-supportive language is the language needed to explain concepts, describe processes, give arguments, etc. It might be generic across most subjects (e.g. *table*, *process*, etc.) or more focused on a particular topic area (e.g. *plants*, *soil*, etc.).

In the third area, EML pedagogy, we identified five key areas of teaching methodology that appear to be particularly important for EML programmes:

- *Adapting to students' L2 proficiency:* this involves teachers being able to use techniques, such as accommodation or convergence, to aid comprehension. It also requires teachers to be able to grade or simplify the language they use in a way that helps L2 students. This includes being able to adapt materials where necessary to make them comprehensible. Teachers need to become skilled in using the students' L1 or translanguaging in a way that supports rather than undermines their development of English skills. For example, Kim et al. (2018) give details of linguistic accommodation, etc., in Korean universities.

- *Supporting the development of students' L2 proficiency:* there are two primary areas to develop in this competency. Firstly, teachers need to be adept at identifying what their students' language learning needs are, i.e. what are they struggling with? Chadwick (2011) highlights the fact that teachers sometimes lack this type of language awareness. Secondly, they need to be able to make use of a range of activities that support language development. For example, if they identify that their students are very slow readers, and that they are getting stuck translating each word in a text, then the teacher needs to know how to set up activities where they are encouraged to work out meanings from the context, and focus on extracting the information needed to answer the question.

- *Building interaction and engagement:* one of the frequent challenges of EML classes is that students become passive and interaction drops significantly. We know that interaction is an important part of the learning process (Fang et al., 2019), and so teachers need to develop skills and techniques for particularly enhancing interaction and engagement. This is partly about having a wider variety of activity types than typically used in an L1 class. But it is also about using activities that require more engagement, such as discovery learning techniques, more Q&A, working in pairs/groups, project work, etc.

- *Developing speaking and writing skills:* students need adequate productive skills (speaking and writing) if they are to be able to show the teacher what they have learned in the subject. Students can naturally find themselves failing in a subject where they have in fact mastered the concepts and skills of the curriculum, but have lacked the productive skills to demonstrate that. Teachers therefore need to focus especially on understanding the components of effective speaking and writing skills – and not get distracted by superficial aspects of spelling and pronunciation, for example.

- *Assessing and feedback:* in many ways, evaluating their students' language skills underpins all the other pedagogy. It requires teachers to understand the aspects of language that impact most on communication, and to have an idea of what level of skill is required at each stage of their students' learning. One important dimension to building interaction is a better awareness of the impact of feedback. The timing and nature of feedback can have a powerful impact on how students react and behave subsequently (Wisniewski et al., 2020).

Summing up

In summary, the success of EML programmes depends heavily on the teaching staff receiving the support and training needed in order to teach a significantly different proposition to L1 programmes. This paper has outlined some of the challenges they face, and the important components of a CPD programme for EML teachers.

Reflection

1. If you are teaching (or have taught) in an EML context, what training and support did you receive? Did it meet your needs? (If you have never taught in such a context, what training do you think you would need?)

2. How might the balance of content and language support vary with the level of the students?

3. Can you summarise the advantages of teaching subject content through English?

4. How can subject teachers and language teachers in your institution collaborate better to help students follow their subject classes in English?

5. If you were the parent of a child who was to be taught subject content through a second language, what questions would you want to ask?

References

Butler, Y. G. (2005). Content-based instruction in EFL contexts: Considerations for effective implementation. *Japan Association for Language Teaching*, 27(2), 227–245.

Cambridge Assessment International Education. (2017). *Bilingual Learners and Bilingual Education*. Cambridge: UCLES. Available at: http://www.cambridgeinternational.org/Images/271190-bilingual-learners-and-bilingual-education.pdf.

Chadwick, T. (2011). *Academic Language Support Across the Curriculum*. Cambridge International Examinations. Bilingual Education Symposium: Key points from presentations, April 2011. Available at: http://www.cambridgeinternational.org/Images/127595-bilingual-education-symposium-april-2011-summary-paper.pdf

Evans, M. (2018). *Advantages of Multilingualism: What is the Impact on School Learning?* Cambridge Education Research Reports. Cambridge: Cambridge University Press.

Fang, J., Tang, L., Yang, J., & Peng, M. (2019). Social interaction in MOOCs: The mediating effects of immersive experience and psychological needs satisfaction. *Telematics and Informatics*, 39, 75–91.

Galloway, N., Numajiri, T., & Rees, N. (2020). The 'internationalisation', or 'Englishisation', of higher education in East Asia. *Higher Education*, 80(3), 395–414.

Galloway, N. (2017). *How Effective is English as a Medium of Instruction (EMI)?* British Council. Available at: https://www.britishcouncil.org/voices-magazine/how-effective-english-medium-instruction-emi

Genesee, F., & Hamayan, E. (2016). *CLIL in Context: Practical Guidance for Educators*. Cambridge: Cambridge University Press.

Hadisantosa, N., Huong, T. T. T., Johnstone, R., Keyuravong, S., & Lee, W. (2010). *Learning Through English: Policies, Challenges and Prospects. Insights from East Asia*. British Council: East Asia. Available at: https://www.teachingenglish.org.uk/sites/teacheng/files/publication_1_-_learning_through_english.pdf

Kim, J., Kim, E. G., & Kweon, S. O. (2018). Challenges in implementing English-medium instruction: Perspectives of Humanities and Social Sciences professors teaching engineering students. *English for Specific Purposes*, 51, 111–123.

Lee, W. (2010). Learning through English: Insights from South Korea. In N. Hadisantosa, T. T. T. Huong, R. Johnstone, S. Keyuravong, W. Lee & R. Johnstone (eds.), *Learning Through English: Policies, Challenges and Prospects* (47–68). British Council: East Asia. Available at: https://www.teachingenglish.org.uk/sites/teacheng/files/publication_1_-_learning_through_english.pdf

Lochmiller, C. R., Lucero, A., & Lester, J. N. (2016). Challenges for a new bilingual program: Implementing the International Baccalaureate Primary Years Programme in four Colombian schools. *Journal of Research in International Education,* 15(2), 155-174.

Mehisto, P. (2012). *Excellence in Bilingual Education: A Guide for School Principals.* Cambridge: Cambridge University Press.

Milligan, L. O., Clegg, J., & Tikly, L. (2016). Exploring the potential for language supportive learning in English medium instruction: A Rwandan case study. *Comparative Education,* 52(3), 328-342.

Pavón Vázquez, V., Avila Lopez, J., Gallego Segador, A., & Espejo Mohedano, R. (2015). Strategic and organisational considerations in planning content and language integrated learning: A study on the coordination between content and language teachers. *International Journal of Bilingual Education and Bilingualism,* 18(4), 409-425.

Thuy, L. N. T. (2016). Reconsidering the first steps of CLIL implementation in Vietnam. *European Journal of Language Policy,* 8(1), 29-56.

Wisniewski, B., Zierer, K., & Hattie, J. (2020). The power of feedback revisited: A meta-analysis of educational feedback research. *Frontiers in Psychology,* 10, 3087.

Yassin, S. M., Marsh, D., Tek, O. E., & Ying. L. Y. (2009). Learners' perceptions towards the teaching of science through English in Malaysia: A quantitative analysis. *International CLIL Research Journal,* 1(2), 54-69.

4 Evaluating the effectiveness of a teacher training programme
Graham Skerritt

Introduction

Cambridge University Press has been working with the Japanese Ministry of Education, Culture, Sports, Science and Technology (MEXT) to provide training for junior and senior high school English teachers all over Japan. This paper describes how the project team investigated the effectiveness of the training programme and the lessons that we learned from this research. The aim of the paper is to share the method we used and the decisions we made, and to provide examples of what we learned, with the aim of helping others to evaluate their own teacher training programmes.

MEXT has introduced several policies to improve English language education in Japan. Among these policies are:

- Introducing English classes at a younger age and increasing the number of hours that children study English.
- Updating university entrance exams so that they also test listening, speaking and writing.
- Encouraging teachers to use a more communicative approach and to use 'active learning' (meaning that students are not just passively receiving information in lecture-style classes).
- Asking teachers to teach lessons in English, as far as possible.

In order to support these policies, MEXT worked with Cambridge University Press to set up and run a teacher training programme for junior and senior high school teachers.

Cambridge University Press also wanted to evaluate the success of the programme so that improvements could be made for future training programmes. One reason that this was of particular interest was that, due to Covid-19, the whole programme was carried out online and thus provided an opportunity to see how effective a fully-online training programme could be in this context.

About the participants

The participants were 551 English teachers from schools all over Japan. Most of these teachers volunteered to do the training, but a small number were asked to take part by their school. The majority (77%) worked in junior high schools (attended by students from ages 12 to 15), whereas the rest (23%) were based in senior high schools (attended by students from ages 15 to 18). All teachers used one of several MEXT-approved coursebooks with their classes.

One challenge of the training programme was to provide content that was interesting and relevant to teachers with very differing levels of experience: 72 had fewer than 3 years' experience, 164 had 3–8 years of experience, 161 had 9–15 years, 69 had 16–20 years, and 85 had more than 20 years' experience (see Figure 4.1).

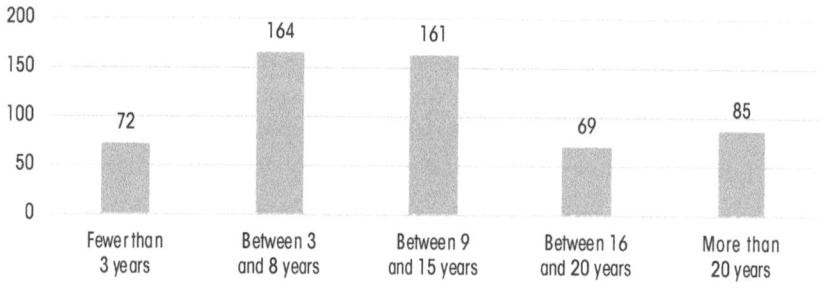

Figure 4.1: Participating teachers' differing levels of experience

Another challenge was that teachers had different levels of confidence in their ability to use computers and participate in online training. The vast majority said they had access to a computer and the internet at school and/or at home – and those that did not, had access to a tablet or smartphone. This suggested that teachers would be able to do the training online, but that some would need support with using the different tools needed.

When designing the programme, we had to keep in mind the different kinds of teachers that would be participating, to make sure that the content was both relevant and understandable for all, and that teachers had easy access to support when they needed it.

About the training programme

A pilot programme that was conducted in 2019 used a combination of in-person seminars, online self-study material, online discussion forums, and assignments that were reviewed by experienced teacher trainers. Although participants expressed satisfaction with the content covered by the 2019 pilot programme, teachers' engagement in online discussion forums was lower than expected – seemingly because they were shy about sharing their ideas and opinions publicly.

For this reason, many teachers did not have a chance to reflect on their learning and try applying it to their own teaching.

As a result of these observations, we made changes to the 2020 programme to encourage more reflection, more trying out of new ideas, and more opportunities to discuss problems and progress with peers.

There were two basic strands to the 2020 programme:

- *Input sessions* (e.g. webinars and online tutorials) that aimed to provide support for challenging areas of teaching. Participants were asked to reflect on these input sessions and note their three key takeaways from each session in a professional development portfolio.

- *Action research* that allowed participants to focus on a particular problem/challenge they wanted to address with a specific group of learners. They were able to use the techniques and activities presented in the input sessions to help with this. They then reflected on the impact of the practices they applied in their portfolios. The inclusion of an individual action research project meant that the teachers with different amounts of teaching experience were able to focus on something that was relevant and interesting to them.

The key components of the course were:

Webinars – interactive presentations led by the course tutors, which focused on different aspects of teaching. The initial webinar was a five-hour training session called the Online Training Event (OTE). Participants were required to attend this live session so they could learn key information about the programme and get started right away. Participants were encouraged to attend the other webinars live too, but recordings were made available for those who needed them.

Tutorials – two one-hour sessions for small groups of six to eight teachers and their tutor. The first tutorial was focused on supporting teachers as they started to apply the insights from the OTE and begin their portfolio assignments. Participants reflected on their teaching contexts and established an area of investigation for the portfolio. The second tutorial asked participants to look back on what they had learned during the programme, particularly through the classroom inquiry that made up the portfolio assignments. They discussed progress, shared reflections, and made plans for future development activity.

A portfolio – a document for the participants to complete over the course of the training programme. The aims of the portfolio were to help participants integrate what they had learned from the different parts of the course, to develop their skills as reflective teachers, and to provide a record of participants' learning during the programme that they could use in the future. It contained 16 short written tasks for the participants to complete. These tasks helped them to identify the aspects of teaching speaking and writing that they most wanted to learn about, conduct the research and reflect on its success. Tutors read participants' portfolios and gave comments and feedback on the first part in November 2020 and on the second part in February 2021. Feedback focused on participants' understanding of key concepts in teaching speaking and writing, their understanding of classroom research skills, and their application of learning from the programme.

Online self-study courses – participants were asked to complete one course between August and November 2020 and the other between December 2020 and January 2021. There was a choice of six courses:

- Background to communicative language teaching
- Developing collaborative learners
- Developing speaking skills
- Developing writing skills
- The role of the teacher
- Using the coursebook.

The schedule for the programme was as follows:

DATE	CONTENT
Aug 2020	• Online Training Event (OTE) – a five-hour online training session including: 1. An introduction to the programme – aims and planning for success. 2. Developing speaking skills and incorporating speaking into your coursebook. 3. Developing writing skills and incorporating writing into your coursebook. 4. Planning your teaching around your coursebook. 5. Next steps: Action research project planning. • Portfolio Tasks 1–2
Sept 2020	• *Optional webinar on online teaching: Synchronous activities* • *Optional webinar on online teaching: Asynchronous activities* • Tutorial #1 • Webinar #1: Meaning-focused tasks • Portfolio Tasks 3–5
Oct 2020	• Webinar #2: Teaching vocabulary for production • Portfolio Tasks 6–7
Nov 2020	• Webinar #3: Assessing learning progress and giving feedback • Portfolio Tasks 9–10 • Tutor feedback on Portfolio Tasks 1–7, 9–10 • Finish online course #1

DATE	CONTENT
Dec 2020	• Webinar #4: Assessment for learning • Portfolio Tasks 8, 11–13
Jan 2021	• Tutorial #2 • Portfolio Tasks 14–16 • Finish online course #2
Feb 2021	• Tutor feedback on Portfolio Tasks 8, 11–16

Table 4.1: The content and schedule for the teacher training programme

Participants were also encouraged to participate in a 'buddy system' that paired them with another teacher and encouraged them to stay in regular contact to update each other on their progress, support each other and share reflections. The goal was to encourage collaboration between teachers that could be continued beyond the training programme.

In order to obtain a certificate of completion, participants needed to complete all the tasks in the portfolio, attend the OTE, attend both tutorials, and complete two online self-study courses. (Since participants could also watch recordings of the four webinars, completion of the portfolio tasks relating to the webinars was taken as evidence of students having watched them.)

Setting up the evaluation measures

To assess the success of the programme, we decided to research these questions:

1. How well did teachers understand effective teaching practices for speaking and writing before taking part in the programme?
2. How well did the training programme improve teachers' use of effective practices for teaching speaking and writing?
3. How well did the training programme improve teachers' confidence at teaching speaking and writing?
4. How well did teachers engage with the training programme?
5. How could the training programme be improved for future use?

In order to examine these questions, we used:

- questionnaires given to participants before and after the training sessions
- interviews with participants
- interviews with the tutors who conducted the training
- portfolio assignments written by the participants
- completion data for the different parts of the programme.

For research questions 1, 2 and 3, we asked the same set of questions about teachers' beliefs and behaviour when teaching speaking and writing – before and after the programme – to see if these changed after participating in the programme. We also created an anonymous post-training feedback questionnaire to ask participants' opinions on the success of the programme.

For research question 4, we mainly consulted data about participation: attendance records for the webinars, completion data from the Learning Management System for the online courses, and whether participants submitted their portfolios or not. We also created a short anonymous questionnaire to send to participants who did not participate, to ask them why they had not engaged, and interviewed some of the participants who failed to complete the programme.

For research question 5, we interviewed tutors and a range of participants (e.g. some who did well, some who seemed to have struggled) to learn more about their experiences and ask for any suggestions they had for improvements. The team running the programme also reflected on this question.

As it was important that all teachers had equal opportunities to learn from the training, it was not feasible to have a control group for this research. However, if we used the same questionnaires in subsequent years, we could make comparisons between the effectiveness of different versions of the programme.

Key findings

> **Research question 1:**
> How well did teachers understand effective teaching practices for speaking and writing before taking part in the programme?

The questions in the pre-training questionnaire were designed to elicit teachers' behaviours and opinions about teaching writing and speaking before they took part in the programme.

The main findings regarding teaching speaking were:

- Although many teachers teach speaking regularly and consistently, some do not.

- When asked about the main purposes of speaking activities, approximately half of the teachers (58%) believed that it was to practise language. This suggests that many teachers may be focusing on accuracy within speaking tasks and could benefit from learning about using fluency building activities and valuing communicative ability.

- The majority of teachers said that they followed what is generally regarded as good practice for choosing which errors to correct by pointing out common errors relating to the target language that were made by several students. However, a few teachers said they avoided error correction (15%) or, conversely, went over all errors (13%).

- With regard to error correction, although 24% reported highlighting errors relating to the language being practised and asking the student to correct it, others reported approaches that are mostly thought of as less successful: 30% asked students to correct all the errors they made, 16% identified and corrected their students' mistakes, 15% said there was an error but not what it was, and 12% asked other students to fix the error.

- Regarding how teachers supported students with speaking activities, some reported behaviours that are widely perceived as good practice: 77% modelled activities, 36% provided a written example, 25% taught functional language to help students and facilitate tasks, and 13% taught functional language to help students check and clarify.

- The biggest problem that teachers reported with teaching speaking was having mixed-level classes (reported by 65% of teachers). However, it's also interesting to note that 30% said they felt their lack of confidence in their own English ability was a problem and that 20% said they just did not know how to teach speaking.

The main findings regarding teaching writing were:

- Surprisingly, teachers with a lower level of English reported teaching writing more often than teachers with a higher level of English, but this may have been because it is easier for them to teach writing than speaking – perhaps because it does not require spontaneous production of spoken language.

- Teachers' responses indicated a range of beliefs about the principal purpose of writing activities: 26% said that it was to communicate a message, 25% said it was to learn the language, 22% said it was to assess students' learning, and 19% said it was to practise grammatical accuracy.

- Some teachers (36%) were the only people to read their students' work. However, 29% of teachers asked students to correct each other's errors and 29% asked students to respond to each other's work. Only 3% used checklists to facilitate peer reviews.

- Regarding their approach to error correction, 37% claimed to correct all their students' errors (which would be very time consuming for teachers and may be demotivating for students), whereas 20% corrected errors relating to the target language. In addition, only a small number flagged errors for students to correct themselves by using underlining of errors (21%) or error codes (5%). After telling students about errors, only 39% asked students to submit a second draft. 44% asked students to make corrections, but didn't check them and 17% did not ask students to correct their errors.

- In order to support writing tasks, many teachers (60%) followed common suggestions of good practice by providing topic ideas, reviewing language that may be useful for the task (47%), or helping students with the structure of the text (24%).

- The most common problems that teachers had with writing was having mixed-level classes (56%) and not having time to correct all their students' errors (49%). As with speaking, lack of confidence in English ability (27%) and lack of knowledge about teaching writing (21%) were also mentioned.

> **Research question 2:**
> How well did the training programme improve teachers' use of effective practices for teaching speaking and writing?

Comparing the answers of participants that completed the programme form, the pre-training questionnaire, and the post-training questionnaire, shows that teachers' behaviours changed in some areas. In many cases, there were only modest changes. However, it's important to remember that changes in behaviour are likely to be very gradual as teachers experiment with new ideas and make decisions about what to incorporate into their practice.

When teaching speaking:

- Participants are focusing on speaking more frequently than before (6% increase in teachers doing speaking every lesson).

- More participants see the purpose of speaking to be building fluency (+13%) rather than practising grammar and vocabulary (-9%).

- A few more participants are asking students to self-correct (+4%) and slightly fewer are asking students to correct mistakes without telling them what it is (-2%) or asking other students to correct their mistakes for them and thus depriving them of an opportunity to self-correct (-1%).

- More participants are teaching students functional language to help them in completing tasks (+8%) and fewer are explaining the activity in Japanese (-3%).

- A lot fewer participants now say they don't know how to teach speaking (-13%), and some are less worried about monitoring all students at once (-7%) or teaching mixed level classes (-3%). This is likely due to the techniques that they have learned on the programme, which could also mean learning from each other or through their own experimentation.

When teaching writing:

- More participants are teaching writing at least once a week (+3%) or a few times a month (+2%) and slightly fewer are never teaching it (-1%) or only assigning it as homework (-1%).
- More participants see the purpose of writing activities as communication (+2%) and fewer see it as a way to practise accuracy (-2%).
- A lot more participants are having students read and respond to each other's work (+11%) or do peer reviews (+6%), and fewer are not having students read each other's work (-8%).
- Although more participants are having students correct each other's work (+5%), slightly more teachers are trying to correct all errors (+1%). This may be because their students are only producing very short texts, but it suggests there may be more room for improving practice here.
- More participants are having students submit a second draft of their work (+10%) rather than asking them to make changes and then not rechecking their work (-10%).
- Fewer participants are explaining tasks in Japanese (-6%) and more are spending time explaining the writing process (+5%) or working on text structure (+2%).
- As a result of these changes, fewer teachers feel they do not know how to teach writing (-10%), or that they do not have time to correct all their students' mistakes (-7%).

Obviously, teachers' responses to the questionnaire only indicate what they say they do rather than what they actually do. It would have been better to triangulate this data with lesson observation analysis to see if they were really putting new ideas into practice. However, since teachers were spread out all over Japan and travel was restricted due to the Covid-19 pandemic, this was not possible.

Research question 3:
How well did the training programme improve teachers' confidence at teaching speaking and writing?

Comparing the answers of participants that completed the programme form, the pre-training questionnaire, and the post-training questionnaire, indicates that teachers' confidence in teaching speaking and writing went up (see Table 4.2).

	VERY CONFIDENT	QUITE CONFIDENT	REASONABLY CONFIDENT	NOT VERY CONFIDENT	NOT AT ALL CONFIDENT
Speaking					
Pre-training	2%	7%	45%	41%	5%
Post-training	4%	18%	50%	26%	3%
Change	▲ 2%	▲ 11%	▲ 5%	▼ 15%	▼ 2%
Writing					
Pre-training	0%	5%	45%	45%	4%
Post-training	3%	11%	52%	30%	3%
Change	▲ 3%	▲ 6%	▲ 7%	▼ 15%	▼ 1%

Table 4.2: Impact of the training programme on teachers' confidence

Participants that completed the programme were also asked if they agreed or disagreed with statements about the course. Responses suggested that the training had had an impact on the participants' confidence and self-efficacy beliefs (see Table 4.3). 83% reported that they believed the course had helped them improve as a teacher. 71% saw the programme as contextually relevant, which may partly be a result of having the ability to choose their own focus for the action research.

	AGREE	NOT SURE	DISAGREE
The training was relevant for me and my situation.	71%	23%	6%
The programme helped me improve as a teacher.	83%	14%	3%
Now I have better techniques for teaching speaking skills.	71%	24%	5%
Now I have better techniques for teaching writing skills.	68%	26%	6%

Table 4.3: Participants' responses to statements about the training programme

Teachers' comments about the course were also very positive and showed how much they had gained from the experience:

> 'I got many tips to improve my English lessons and it was a great opportunity to reflect upon. I would like to incorporate what I learned through this programme into my classes.'

> 'I can see [my students] improvement on their English, especially speaking and writing skills.'

The tutors also believed that the programme was a success. They commented that 'everyone learned something' and that the participants who put a lot of effort in showed 'significant evidence of learning'. They also believed that the programme 'opened participants' minds to different ways of teaching' and 'made them think a lot more about what they do and why they do it'. In fact, one tutor concluded that 'all teachers should be doing [the programme]'.

> **Research question 4:**
> How well did teachers engage with the training programme?

Of the 551 teachers that signed up for the programme, 428 completed it – a completion rate of 78%. This compares very favourably to estimates of average completion rates for online courses, which some have estimated as between 15% (Jordan, 2015) for free courses and 78% (WCET, 2013) for compulsory courses that are part of a degree.

The engagement rate for different parts of the course was also higher than 80% for most parts of the course (see Table 4.4).

PART OF THE COURSE	NUMBER OF TEACHERS ATTENDING	%
Online Training Event	508	94%
Tutorial 1	528	96%
Portfolio Part 1	472	86%
Online Course 1	461	83%
Tutorial 2	479	87%
Portfolio Part 2	439	80%
Online Course 2	456	83%

Table 4.4: The engagement rate for different parts of the training programme

> Note: Approximately 70% of teachers attended the webinars live, but since teachers could watch recordings at a later date, a higher number than 70% engaged with this content.

The 123 participants who did not complete the programme were sent an anonymous questionnaire to ask for feedback about why they did not engage. We received responses from 30 people, and by far the most common answer (80%) was lack of time. This was reflected in the comments from interviews with participants who either struggled to complete the course or dropped out.

It is also worth remembering that this training programme took place during the Covid-19 pandemic, and this may have caused some people to have less time for training. It may also have affected participants' overall stress levels and receptiveness to taking part in a training programme. Those teachers who did complete the programme did very well to stay focused in these challenging times.

> **Research question 5:**
> How could the training programme be improved for future use?

Ensure teachers have time for training

The biggest reason that teachers gave for not being able complete the course was lack of time. This was shown in the questionnaire results and reflected in teachers' comments about the programme:

> *'[I didn't participate because of] a scheduling problem: lessons, meetings, parent consultations, and extracurricular activities in weekdays and weekends meant that I was just too busy.'*

This and similar comments show that several teachers struggled to fit the training in alongside their other responsibilities. Ideally, teachers need to be given time within working hours to complete the programme – perhaps by temporarily excusing them from some of their other duties. However, if this is not possible, the programme should take care to be sensitive to teacher's busy periods when assigning tasks and setting deadlines.

Provide basic computer training for teachers

Cambridge University Press had to provide a lot of technical support for teachers. In fact, some teachers had very little knowledge about using computers – for example, they did not know how to attach files to an email, type a URL into their browser, or send helpful inquiry emails (e.g. they did not always use the email address that they had registered with, and often did not give their name or the name of their school). There were also problems with emails not being received by teachers because messages ended up in their junk folders. This could be avoided by teacher's adding relevant addresses to their contact list.

To help smooth the running of the programme, it would be beneficial for teachers who are less confident with technology to receive some basic IT training before starting the programme.

Include additional support on action research

Several tutors commented that participants found it difficult to understand the concept of action research and suggested that more support with this was necessary. Additional webinars may be the best way to do this, as they were particularly well liked because participants with a lower level of English could rewatch them if they did not understand everything the first time.

Refer to the coursebooks that the teachers are using

Many of the tutors felt that participants struggled to understand how to apply the ideas from the webinars and the online courses to their own teaching contexts, because they needed to see examples from the coursebooks they were using with their classes. This is a little more complicated than it sounds, because not all teachers use the same coursebook.

Reconceptualise the buddy system

The buddy system was a good idea for encouraging teachers to share ideas and continue their development outside of the scheduled training sessions. However, not as many people used it as was hoped. One reason was that teachers felt uncomfortable contacting people they did not know well. Another reason was that teachers did not have clear reasons to contact each other or particular topics that they needed to discuss. Without a clear structure, participants were not motivated to contact each other.

To solve this problem, the buddy system could include project work that the teachers need to complete together. In fact, the Lesson Study approach, which originated with mathematics classes in Japan, could provide a structure for the buddy system. In Lesson Study, teachers meet and plan a lesson together. Then, one teacher teaches the lesson and the others observe. This means that the teacher being observed feels less pressure, because the observers are evaluating the plan that they created together, so the focus is on the plan rather than the teacher. After the lesson, the group meets to evaluate the lesson and reflect on what they may do differently next time. (See Doig and Groves, 2011, for a more detailed description of the Lesson Study approach.) In other words, it is a group action research project, which should fit well with the approach taken by this programme – particularly because Lesson Study is a Japanese idea.

Provide English training

Many participants were keen to improve their English ability. This provides an opportunity for teachers to experience the communicative ideas being presented from the perspective of a student. By learning in this way, teachers can understand more about how the techniques can be applied and reflect on how they could be used in their own classrooms.

In fact, considering that those with a higher level of English seemed to get more out of the training programme, perhaps the first step in future programmes should be to assess participants' language levels and then offer language development courses to those with a lower level than B2. This could be completed before the training programme.

Conclusion

The goal of the training programme was to increase participants' skills and confidence at teaching speaking and writing, in order to follow the guidelines from MEXT regarding English education in Japan. Overall, analysis of the programme suggests that it was a success: a high percentage of the 551 teachers that started the programme completed it (78%), most of these teachers (89%) said they would use the ideas from the programme with their classes, and a large number (66%) reported that the programme had made them more confident at teaching English.

Before the programme, many teachers were not following good practice for teaching speaking and writing in a communicative way. For example, when teaching speaking, many teachers focused on accuracy and relied on the use of Japanese to set up and run activities. Additionally, when teaching writing, many teachers were reluctant to do activities because they worried about not having time to check all of their students' written work. However, following the programme, teachers are starting to apply the techniques they learned. They understand the importance of focusing on fluency in speaking tasks and of teaching students functional language to help them work together. They are also starting to ask students to read and comment on each other's written work. These changes in behaviour suggest that teachers are gradually beginning to try out and adopt the ideas from the programme.

The project to evaluate the programme provided us with a lot of good data that we could use to track teachers' involvement and progress. Conducting interviews with teachers and tutors was also very useful as it allowed us to hear more detailed answers about their opinions of the programme. Conducting lesson observations would also have been very useful, but unfortunately this was not possible. Another data point we could consider in the future is getting students' feedback on their lessons, to see how they react to new ideas and teaching techniques.

Reflection

For managers

1. What are the most important development needs of the teachers you manage?
2. One of the recommendations here was to 'reconceptualise the buddy system' to encourage teachers to work together. How might you help teachers to set up communities of practice so that they can lend support, help and guidance to each other?
3. How might you monitor the effectiveness of a teacher development programme both during delivery and after delivery?

For teachers

1. How important is the development of productive skills to your learners?
2. Do you feel that enough time is devoted to productive skills development in your teaching context?
3. This course was delivered online. Have you experienced online teacher development? If so, what were the advantages? Was there anything that you did not like about it?

References

Doig, B., & Groves, S. (2011). Japanese lesson study: Teacher professional development through communities of inquiry. *Mathematics Teacher Education and Development,* 13(1), 77–93. Available at: https://files.eric.ed.gov/fulltext/EJ960950.pdf

Jordan, K. (2015). MOOC Completion Rates: The Data. [Weblog post]. Available at: http://www.katyjordan.com/MOOCproject.html

WCET. (2013). Managing Online Education 2013: Practices in Ensuring Quality – Executive Summary. *WCET*. Available at: https://wcet.wiche.edu/wp-content/uploads/sites/11/2021/07/2013ManagingOnlineEducationSurveyExecutiveSummary.pdf

Section 2: Inclusivity, differentiation and learning strategies

5 Differentiation by design – optimising learning in the English language classroom

Betsy Parrish

Introduction

In the Cambridge University Press (2018) world teacher survey of over 10,000 teachers, 41% reported that managing mixed-ability classes is the most challenging aspect of the job. Mixed ability is not just about language proficiency, though; it encompasses prior school experiences, cultural influences, attitudes about teaching and learning, levels of digital competence and personal circumstances. The fact is, mixed-ability classes are a reality in every classroom and should not be seen as a deterrent to learning. One might even argue that the range of backgrounds and abilities of learners in our classes allows for richer interactions and multiple perspectives, peer teaching and multifaceted learning.

In any classroom, some students participate all the time, while others are non-communicative, which can lead teachers to think that they lack skills in English.

> 'Sometimes, for example, we assume that the silent student doesn't understand when in fact the listening skills may be quite strong. Similarly, confident speech may mask very limited literacy skills.'
> (Bell, 2012: 88)

Reticence to participate should not be attributed to a lack of willingness to learn or to levels of competence; the outward behaviours of students may have as much to do with experiential and affective factors as they do with language proficiency (Carter and Henrichsen, 2015). Learners' views of student and teacher roles can also affect levels of participation. For example, students coming from educational systems that favour lecture-based teaching or where collaborative learning is rare, need to adjust to a language classroom that relies heavily on pair and group work. We should expand the notion of mixed ability to include a wide range of factors that contribute to what Tomlinson and Imbeau (2010) call a *learner profile*.

LEARNER PROFILE

Readiness: How well prepared are learners for the content, skills, and language demands of classroom tasks?

Interest: What content, knowledge, and skills will be of most interest to learners and, by extension, motivate them?

Affect: How might learner attitudes, emotions, or feelings affect learning?

Learning profile: How do learners approach learning? How might learning preferences or cultural expectations about teaching and learning roles vary among learners?

(Tomlinson and Imbeau, 2010: 16–17)

No two learners are alike

The contexts of English language teaching around the world are as varied as the learners that are in those classes learning English. No two students are the same, even in contexts that appear to be more linguistically or culturally homogeneous. Consider these scenarios. Which is most similar to the context in which you currently work as an English language educator?

> Hoa teaches an English class with 40 students at a technical university in Hanoi, Vietnam. Her students are mostly computer science majors who are taking English as a requirement for graduation. The textbook they use is a general English course, with little focus on English for technical purposes.

> Laura teaches an intermediate-level English class with 15 adults at a private language school in Toronto. Most of the learners are young adults who would like to improve their English for work or for entering university in Canada. Some are newcomers to Canada with credentials from their country and some are international students.

> Ignacio teaches in a new CLIL programme at a primary school in Valencia, Spain, and is the teacher for the science modules taught to 10 to 11-year-old learners. In this class, they explore topics such as the water cycle, states of matter, landscapes, and ecosystems. The students are at the A1 level and have explored some of these topics in their science curriculum in Spanish in earlier grade levels.

> Oscar teaches a group of adult immigrants at a programme in Melbourne, Australia, housed in a neighbourhood library. Learners in his class come from Thailand, China, Iran, Syria and Burma. Some have credentials from their home country and some have interrupted formal schooling, with minimal literacy in their first language.

The children in Ignacio's class may not be used to learning science content in English, but they bring background from having learned some of the topics in earlier grades and this affects their *readiness* to learn science in English. Hoa's learners may have many different *interests* outside of their major that she could draw on during instruction. Some of Oscar's students have been in refugee camps and some have experienced the trauma of war, perhaps impacting their *affect* in the classroom. Laura's students, like Oscar's, most likely bring many different *learning profiles* because of their wide range of educational experiences from different countries. In each of these contexts, every learner brings unique needs, expectations, preferences for ways of learning, background knowledge and skills to English language classes.

Language and skills for success in today's world

As educators, our job is to provide a classroom environment that gives all learners equal access to the content and learning in our classes. The answer to supporting the range of learner profiles in any class is *differentiation*.

> 'In differentiated classrooms, teachers ensure that students compete against themselves as they grow and develop more than they compete against one another, always moving toward—and often beyond—designated content goals.'
>
> (Tomlinson, 2014: 4)

What is differentiation?

With a set of clear learning outcomes in mind for a lesson or unit of instruction, the *content*, *process* and *products* (or assessments of learning) are adjusted to help all learners progress in their language development in ways that are in keeping with their abilities and needs (Tomlinson and Imbeau, 2010). Here we look more closely at what it means to differentiate the content, process and products of instruction; these elements of differentiation can be applied in any classroom setting.

COMPONENTS OF DIFFERENTIATION

Content: What do learners need to know and understand? This can include content knowledge, such as environmental studies, maths or psychology, as well as the language learners need to be successful in a lesson/unit, for example, language functions and forms, or academic vocabulary.

Process: What instructional approach and classroom tasks allow learners to make sense of the content? As teachers, how can we modify our practices or provide multiple inroads to success?

Product: How do learners demonstrate what they have learned? What kinds of assessments do we use? Are there multiple options that draw on all language skills and a variety of modalities, e.g. print, digital, aural/oral?

(Tomlinson and Imbeau, 2010: 15)

Research suggests that while teachers may understand the concept of differentiation and believe in its importance, they do not necessarily know how to apply the principles in their classes (Joseph, 2013).

Maintaining rigour in the differentiated classroom

One misconception that many educators have is that differentiating instruction automatically means lowering expectations for some learners (Blackburn, 2019). Differentiation does not mean lowering the bar for some; in fact, it's just the opposite. By adjusting our practices in keeping with learner profiles, more students – not fewer – are likely to meet learning outcomes in our lessons when given the opportunity to demonstrate learning in multiple ways.

As we will see, differentiation often leads to more productive team work, deeper exploration and critical thinking about the topics at hand, and improved communication – all central to the 21st-century skills we know to be essential for success in today's world, as shown in Figure 5.4 (Parrish, 2015; Cambridge University Press, 2020). The goal of differentiation is to help all learners achieve at their highest potential. It is our job as educators to determine the kind of scaffolding and supports different learners need to achieve learning outcomes (Blackburn, 2019).

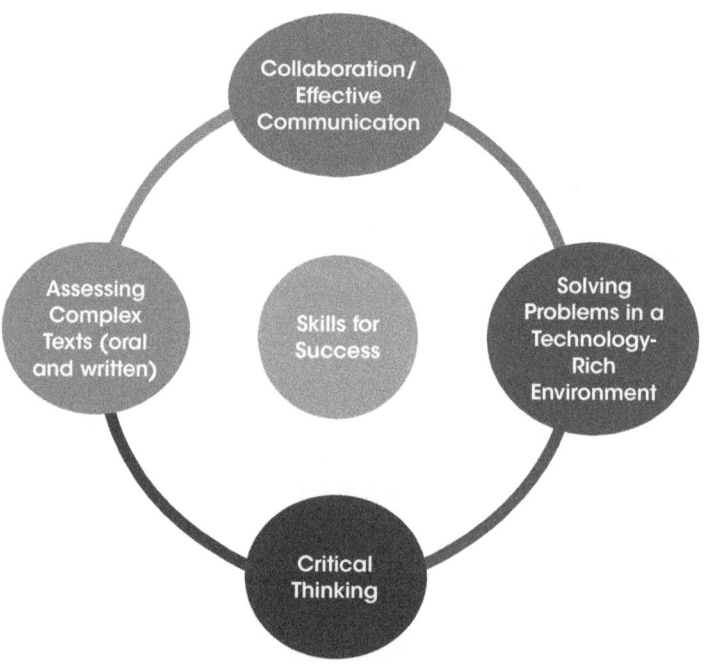

Figure 5.4: Skills for success in the twenty-first century (adapted from Parrish, 2015; Cambridge University Press, 2020)

Starting the differentiation process

In order to determine the ways in which the teacher needs to differentiate instruction, we start by examining the content, process and product of a task or lesson (or even a whole unit of instruction).

- What language, skills, and knowledge do learners need in order to be successful with the tasks in this lesson?
- How will learners with varying learner profiles go about meeting the lesson outcomes?
- What will the teacher assess? (We could assess learners' success with the learning processes, for example, their participation in a debate, or we could assess the products or artifacts of learning, such as posters, essays or formal presentations.)

By doing this analysis of lesson demands, the teacher can determine the kinds of adjustments needed so that all learners can contribute fully to the lesson (Parrish, 2019).

A critical stage in every lesson is purposeful pre-assessment, in order to identify where learners may have the most overlaps in terms of readiness, interest and learning profiles with the content we are planning to teach; then, we can gear the lesson to the needs of learners (Tomlinson, 2017). Providing a wide variety of tasks types at this pre-assessment stage allows learners to demonstrate what they know in ways that are accessible to them (Oberg, 2010). Pre-assessments can include: K-W-L charts (what do you Know, what do you Want to learn, what did you Learn); short surveys; brief goal setting with 'can-do' statements related to objectives of the lesson; four corners with images of outcomes to be achieved in a unit of study, instructing students to stand in the corners representing: 1) what they can do, and; 2) what they need to do (Parrish, 2019).

Differentiating the content

Research suggests that teachers are most hesitant to differentiate the *content* of their lessons (Tzanni, 2018), perhaps because it seems to be the most time-consuming element to differentiate. Drawing on the principles of the *Language Experience Approach*, where a class co-constructs a text starting with learners' oral language, we can use learner-generated content to differentiate for varying levels of learner readiness and interest. Imagine a lesson in the curriculum on likes and dislikes with pre-determined topics. Instead, have students start the lesson by sharing photos of their weekend activities or, as in Figure 5.5, use the whiteboard function in an online class so that learners can build content in multiple ways; then, use the content generated as the basis of the lesson.

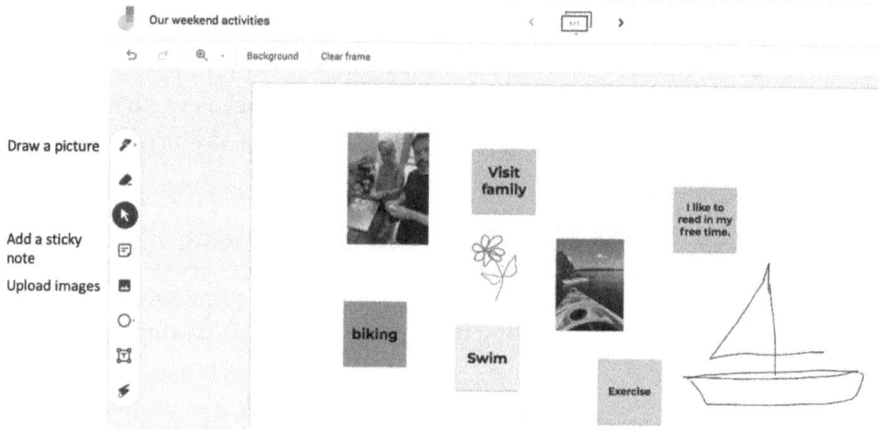

Figure 5.5: Generating learner content

The Jigsaw Approach, where different learners are assigned different portions of a text or different texts on the same topic, is another very effective way to differentiate for *content*. Texts on different themes, levels of complexity and expertise, and different formats (e.g. infographics, blog posts, articles), or modalities (e.g. print, audio, video), can be used in the same lesson. Jigsaw also relates to *process*, as it can lighten the reading or listening load in a lesson, and it prompts practice with multiple language skills as learners present what they learned to others.

Differentiating the process

Differentiating for *process* is all about the instructional decisions we make, some of which inherently lead to differentiation by design. For example, asking everyone to read a story and answer a set of comprehension questions favours the faster reader; the language in the questions is fixed and most often has a pre-determined answer. Instead, if learners are asked to read and complete a linear string graphic organiser, as shown in Figure 5.6, noting events that unfolded in the story, they can record ideas using the language they know yet still demonstrate understanding of a text.

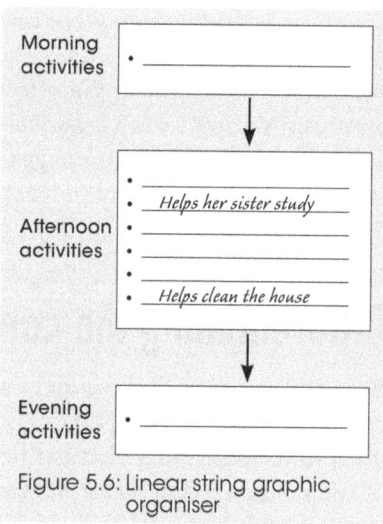

Figure 5.6: Linear string graphic organiser

The overall teaching approach we choose also affects the ease with which we can differentiate for differing learner profiles. Strengths-based approaches that place the learner at the centre of instruction will naturally lead to greater levels of learner choice in a lesson (Parrish, 2019). Communicatively-based approaches that contextualise linguistic input and promote negotiated interactions among learners will more naturally address varying learner profiles than a highly teacher-centred approach.

Project-based learning (PBL) is a highly learner-centred and student-driven approach that is particularly well suited for differentiation. In PBL, learners develop their own lines of inquiry, choose their roles on a team, and work towards developing different products. Project-based learning may also lead to greater intrinsic motivation as learners select materials that are in keeping with their interests, abilities and levels of content knowledge (Bell, 2010).

Let's look at some typical classroom tasks and think about adjustments we can make in our *process*.

TYPICAL CLASSROOM TASKS	ADJUSTMENTS THAT LEAD TO DIFFERENTIATION FOR LEARNER READINESS, INTERESTS OR LEARNING PROFILES
Reading a text or listening to lectures or presentations, and answering a list of comprehension questions	• Assign every other question to each half of the class. This lightens the load and has the added benefit of prompting speaking practice when students are paired up to share what they found for their items. • Have learners read or listen and complete a graphic organiser based on text genre: a timeline for a biography or historical account; a T-chart for a compare/contrast or cause-effect text; a flow chart for a process text or a problem/solutions text. Open-ended tasks like this allow learners to demonstrate understanding at their own level. Completing graphic organisers while listening or reading has the added benefit of helping learners to see the structure of a text.
Essay writing using the process-writing approach	• Provide multiple means of pre-writing, including interactive speaking activities to generate topics and content. Build learners' oral language first by providing oral language frames tied to the writing purpose (e.g. argumentation, cause-effect) as a bridge to writing (Egan and Parrish, 2019). • Provide paragraph frames or writing templates as scaffolds for writing. Graff and Birkenstein (2014) suggest that providing these templates allows learners to shape their ideas more effectively.
Discussion activities	• Assign roles based on learner strengths, e.g. scribe, manager, timekeeper, reporter. In project-based learning, those roles could include 'the numbers person', if there is any analysis of data involved; artist; 'computer whiz'– the one who is most comfortable using digital tools, etc. • Provide language frames needed for collaboration; consider the language functions needed to sustain a meaningful discussion: asking for and giving opinions; clarifying; elaborating, synthesising ideas generated.

Most of us think ...
We seem to agree that ...

TYPICAL CLASSROOM TASKS	ADJUSTMENTS THAT LEAD TO DIFFERENTIATION FOR LEARNER READINESS, INTERESTS OR LEARNING PROFILES
Paired interview (commonly found as pre-reading/ listening; as a practice activity in text books)	• Use one-question survey: assign one question to two to four students, have them mingle (or use breakout rooms online) to talk to everyone in class, and take notes or tally responses. In teams, learners analyse the information gathered to prompt high-order thinking. For example, after reading studies on the science of happiness, learners conduct a one-question survey by selecting a question, such as one of these: **Post-reading/follow-up** T: *Let's do our own research. Which of the happiness enhancers are people in class most likely to try? Interview everyone in class with your assigned question and tally your results.* 1. How likely are you to try the Gratitude Journal? Very Likely to Try It Likely to Try It Somewhat Likely to Try It Not at All Likely to Try It 2. How likely are you to try Performing Acts of Kindness? Very Likely to Try It Likely to Try It Somewhat Likely to Try It Not at All Likely to Try It (Parrish, 2019: 159–160)
Grammar presentations	• Lead learners to a grammar point through context and co-construct rules together; this allows more learners to demonstrate their understanding of forms presented as compared to introducing grammar forms deductively and in charts. For example, to teach comparative forms, share real-world data on a topic of interest or one in your curriculum (such as expenses, preferences, jobs trends) and then lead learners to make comparisons based on what they see to teach comparative forms. Reformulate their ideas as needed to present the target forms, for example: *People spend <u>considerably more</u> on healthcare <u>than</u> on transportation.* *There are <u>far more</u> jobs in healthcare <u>than</u> in education.*
Research projects	• Use project-based learning (PBL) in lieu of individual research projects. • Differentiate PBL teams based on any number of factors, for example, learners' interests, content knowledge, reading level, and/or leadership skills.

Table 5.1: Adjustments that can be made to typical classroom tasks, that lead to differentiation for learner readiness, interests or learning profiles

Differentiating the products

The first step to designing differentiated *products* is determining exactly what it is that we would like to assess. Imagine you were completing a unit on endangered species that includes the following content:

Concepts: endangered species; wild animals; conservation

Language functions:

- Ask for and give opinion.
- Describe possible solutions.

Language forms:

- Modals for making recommendation (*companies should ...*, *governments can ...*, etc.)
- Expressions for cause/effect (*because of*, *due to*, etc.)

Vocabulary: *endangered, extinct, species, habitat, overfishing, destroy, protect*

Critical thinking skills:

- Evaluate the causes of endangerment and extinction of animals; identify and evaluate solutions.

This unit ends with the following collaborative task:

> **COLLABORATION**
>
> **8 A** Work in a small group. Choose an endangered species and make a fact sheet about it. Include the following information:
> - Description of its habitat
> - Threats or dangers to it
> - Ways to protect it
> - Photos of the animal and its habitat
>
> **B** Present your fact sheets to the class. As a class, choose an endangered species to sponsor.

(Baker and Westbrook, 2018)

Creating a fact sheet is one perfectly effective way to assess learning from the unit. What roles will learners take on in the process of developing the fact sheet? Which learner strengths does this task privilege? How could learners with strong oral skills, but perhaps more limited literacy skills, demonstrate mastery of the content and language in the unit? Table 5.2 gives examples of some of the ways we can work with existing tasks in our textbooks and curricula, and make small adjustments in order to reach a broader range of learner profiles.

STEPS OF FINAL PRODUCT IN THE TEXTBOOK	APPLYING THE DIFFERENTIATION PRINCIPLES
Work in a small group and choose an endangered species.	• Small groups of students first generate lists of possible species on poster paper (or a whiteboard online); students read all the lists and place a check/tick next to the two of most interest to them. The results are used to establish teams based on interest (and, potentially, readiness). • Students choose roles they will take on in the process of completing this task: online researcher, print researcher, artist, writer, project manager, etc.
Make a fact sheet about the endangered species. Include the following information: • description of its habitat • threats or dangers to it • ways to protect it • photos of the animal and its habitat.	Provide multiple options to demonstrate learning, including the same information as in the original task. Learners could: • create a podcast about this endangered species • create an info-graphic • make a video of a mock TV show (interviewing the experts) or a public service announcement • create a poster for a campaign on saving this endangered species.
Present your fact sheets to the class.	Provide alternatives to whole-group presentations, for example: • Develop a jigsaw reading task using the class-generated products. • Have the class generate a list of questions they would like to ask one another about their project. • Conduct a gallery walk (half the class stationed with their products and half the class circulating to view and learn; then switch those roles).

Table 5.2: Examples for applying the differentiation principles to existing tasks, to reach a broader range of learner profiles

Notice that none of the alternative products take additional preparation time for the teacher. Any assessment rubric or checklist the teacher might use for the fact sheet could be used equally well for any of the alternate products. Replacing whole-group presentations with collaborative means of presenting the information promotes practice with effective interpersonal communication.

As shown in the examples in this chapter, final products and assessments can take many forms. Providing these multiple options in our classes acknowledges differing readiness, interest, affect and learning profiles. Figure 5.7 highlights these options with additional examples proposed by Parrish (2019).

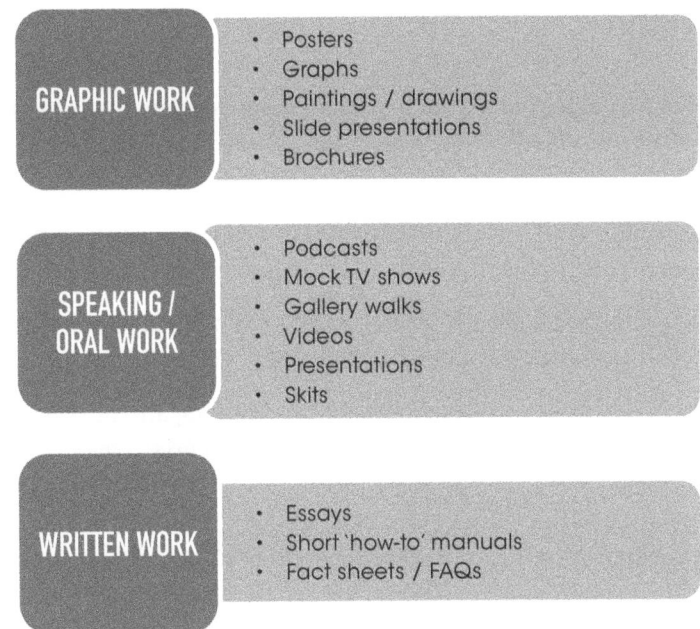

Figure 5.7: Types of products to assess learning outcomes (Parrish, 2019: 221–222)

Conclusion

Differentiating the content, process and product(s) of every unit is not realistic, but being attentive at all times and making even small adjustments is. Prioritise what you may have the most control over in your setting. If you are bound by a set curriculum, modifying the content may be less feasible. However, you can modify the approach you take to implementing that curriculum.

Thinking back to the scenarios of the four classes from around the world, conducting interest surveys and using learner-generated content in lessons is a way that Hoa can motivate learners taking a required English class at a technical university. Jigsaw tasks or one-question surveys may appeal to the students in Laura's class, as those instructional practices automatically promote effective communication and teamwork, skills needed in work and academic settings. Ignacio's students in the CLIL science class could carry out project-based learning to explore a wide range of aspects of climate change. Varying the types of products, those that focus on oral language rather than writing, may support the emergent readers in Oscar's class for newcomer adults. This kind of differentiation by design will optimise learning for all in the English language classroom.

Reflection

1. Considering the learners that you serve, how do individuals vary in their learner profiles?

2. Again, considering your learners, where do you see the greatest need for differentiation: the content of your lessons, your teaching process, or the types of products you assign as assessments? Explain your thinking.

3. In which dimension does it seem easiest to implement differentiation? And which is the most challenging?

4. Is it feasible to develop an action plan for applying any of these principles of differentiation? What would be the first steps?

References

Baker, L. R., & Westbrook, C. (2018). *Prism Reading, Level 2*. Cambridge: Cambridge University Press.

Bell, J. (2012). Teaching mixed level classes. In A. Burns & J. C. Richards (eds.), *The Cambridge Guide to Pedagogy and Practice in Second Language Teaching* (86–94). New York: Cambridge University Press.

Bell, S. (2010). Project-based learning for the 21st century: Skills for the future. *The Clearing House: A Journal of Educational Strategies, Issues and Ideas,* 83(2), 39–43. https://doi.org/10.1080/00098650903505415

Blackburn, B. R. (2019). *Rigor and Differentiation in the Classroom: Tools and Strategies.* New York: Routledge. https://doi.org/10.4324/9781351185912

Cambridge University Press. (2020). *Cambridge Life Competencies: An Introduction.* Cambridge: Cambridge University Press. Available at: https://issuu.com/cambridgeupelt/docs/cambridgelifecompetencies_introductionbooklet_issu

Cambridge University Press. (2018). *World Teacher Survey*. Cambridge: Cambridge University Press. Available at: https://www.cambridge.org/elt/blog/2018/12/07/world-teacher-survey-results/

Carter, S. J. & Henrichsen, L. E. (2015). Addressing reticence: The challenge of engaging reluctant adult ESL students. *Journal of Adult Education,* 44(2), 15–20.

Egan, P., & Parrish, B. (2019). Oral language as a bridge to academic writing. In K. Schaetzel, J. K. Peyton & R. Fernández (eds.), *Preparing Adult English Learners to Write for College and the Workplace.* Ann Arbor: University of Michigan Press.

Graff, G., & Birkenstein, C. (2014). *They Say, I Say: The Moves that Matter in Academic Writing* (3rd edition). New York: W.W. Norton and Company, Inc.

Joseph, S. (2013). Differentiating instruction: Experiences of pre-service and in-service trained teachers. *Caribbean Curriculum,* 20, 31–51.

Oberg, C. (2010). Guiding classroom instruction through performance assessment. *Journal of Case Studies in Accreditation and Assessment,* 1, 1–11. Available at: http://www.aabri.com/manuscripts/09257.pdf.

Parrish, B. (2019). *Teaching Adult English Language Learners: A Practical Introduction.* (2nd edition). Cambridge: Cambridge University Press.

Parrish, B. (2015). Meeting the language needs of today's adult English language learner: Issue brief. *LINCS ESL Pro Project.* Washington DC: US Department of Education, Office of Career, Technical and Adult Education. Available at: https://lincs.ed.gov/state-resources/federal-initiatives/esl-pro

Tomlinson, C. A. (2017). *How to Differentiate Instruction in Academically Diverse Classrooms* (3rd edition). Alexandria: ASCD. Available at: https://files.ascd.org/staticfiles/ascd/pdf/siteASCD/publications/books/HowtoDifferentiateInstructioninAcademicallyDiverseClassrooms-3rdEd.pdf

Tomlinson, C. A. (2014). *The Differentiated Classroom: Responding to The Needs of All Learners* (2nd edition). Alexandria: ASCD.

Tomlinson, C. A., & Imbeau, M. B. (2010). *Leading and Managing a Differentiated Classroom.* Alexandria: ASCD.

Tzanni, V. (2018). Exploring differentiated instruction in TESOL: The teachers' beliefs and practices in Greece. *Research Papers in Language Teaching and Learning,* 9(1), 149–165.

6 Specific learning difficulties and inclusive language teaching material design

Judit Kormos

Introduction

The diversity of language learners has long been recognised in the field of second language learning. Learners with Specific Learning Difficulties (SpLDs), such as dyslexia (reading difficulties), dysgraphia (writing difficulties), dyscalculia (numerical difficulties) and dyspraxia (difficulties with fine-motor skills), constitute a large group of students who might need support in learning additional languages. In fact, one out of ten students is quite likely to exhibit signs of SpLDs (Butterworth and Kovas, 2013), which may exert a significant influence on how additional languages are learned. Therefore, in order to design effective language teaching programmes and materials, it is essential to take the needs and strengths and weaknesses of language learners with SpLDs into account.

Inclusive learning environments

The needs of students with SpLDs are best met in an inclusive learning environment. For inclusion to be successful, the difficulties with language learning experienced by students should be identified, the obstacles removed and appropriate support provided. For successful inclusion, it is also important to ensure that teaching materials are accessible to everyone. This aim is embodied in the concept of *Universal Design for Learning* (Center for Applied Special Technology, 2019), which helps to provide flexibility in the context of education and allows accessibility to the curriculum and educational materials for all learners.

Universal Design for Learning

Universal Design for Learning has three main principles:

1. The first principle states that we should give learners different opportunities and choices to access information (visually – as in reading, or aurally – as in listening).

2. The second principle recommends that multiple means of action and expression should be offered when students practise what they learned or demonstrate their knowledge in tests. For example, these different means for expression can involve physical action, and choices between writing and speaking.

3. The third principle highlights the importance of using different ways of engaging students, arousing their interest, maintaining their motivation and helping them manage their own learning, with appropriate learning strategies.

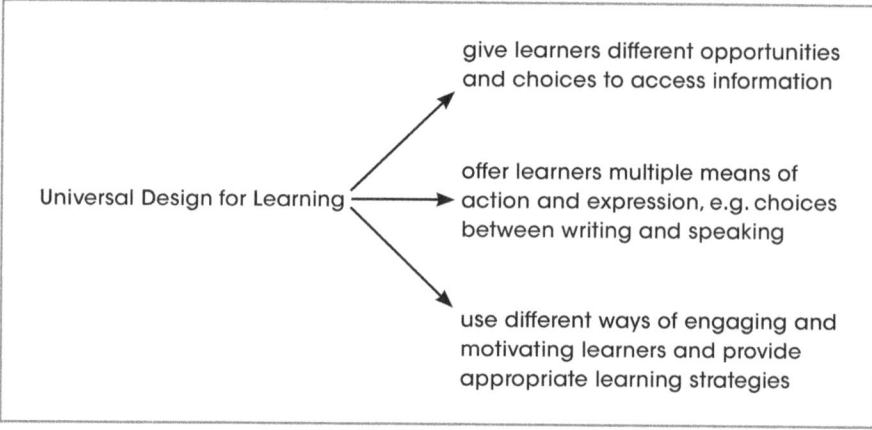

Figure 6.1: The three main principles of Universal Design for Learning

Materials design

In designing inclusive language teaching materials that take into account the needs of students with SpLDs, it is of great importance to ensure that students can access input texts in different modes, and that they can make their own choice about which mode best supports their learning. For example, if possible, texts should be presented in three formats: as a reading text, as a listening text, or possibly as a video recording with captions or a downloadable transcript.

Another requirement for SpLD-friendly materials design is that materials on a page should be arranged so that they appear uncluttered and are easy to navigate. Many learners with SpLDs prefer sans serif fonts and larger spaces between words and lines. For this reason, it is useful to provide modified large print versions of coursebooks and teaching materials to aid visual processing. In digital teaching tools, options for students to adjust font size, line spacing and background and font colour should also be offered.

The addition of audio-visual material, illustrations, pictures and mind maps to accompany written texts is helpful for students with SpLDs. However, care needs to be taken not to create visual overload, and illustrations should carry meaning rather than be just purely decorative. Colour coding and visual enhancement can also direct the attention of students with SpLDs to key information in instructions and to language presented in tasks. Nonetheless, it is important to bear in mind that colour or visual enhancement should not be the only mode of conveying information, as it might disadvantage students with visual impairments and colour perception problems.

Every student, including those with SpLDs, benefits from clear, concise explanations of task instructions. Breaking down these explanations into stages or steps, as well as demonstrating how to solve a task, aids students' understanding of what is required of them and helps to engage them in language learning activities that support their development.

Summing up

The need for inclusivity in our classrooms seems axiomatic and therefore we need to ensure that, wherever possible, we apply these basic principles of materials design so that we offer the best possible opportunities to all our learners.

References

Butterworth, B., & Kovas, Y. (2013). Understanding neurocognitive developmental disorders can improve education for all. *Science*, 340(6130), 300–305. Available at: https://www.science.org/doi/abs/10.1126/science.1231022

About Universal Design for Learning. (2019). Center for Applied Special Technology. Available at: http://www.cast.org/our-work/about-udl.html#.XyHq1vhKjfZ

7 Language learning strategies
Karen Forbes

What are language learning strategies?

Research into the field of language learning strategies started in the mid-1970s and continues to flourish and evolve today. While much of the early work in this area focused on identifying and classifying the strategies used by 'successful' language learners, the focus quickly shifted to exploring effective ways to teach students to develop effective strategies in the classroom.

Language learning strategies are generally considered as a means of ensuring that language is stored, retained and able to be produced when necessary or, as Griffiths (2018: 19) succinctly puts it, they are 'actions chosen by learners for the purpose of language learning'. Strategies, as such, generally involve some degree of consciousness. They can be used across a range of different skill areas (e.g. speaking, listening, reading, writing, vocabulary learning, grammar) and also have a variety of different functions. The most common functions are:

- *Cognitive:* Involves mental processing of the language, for example, inferring the meaning of an unknown word in a text.
- *Metacognitive:* Involves more deliberately planning how to use a strategy, monitoring its effectiveness or evaluating its use, for example, goal-setting.
- *Social:* Involves engaging in interaction with others, for example, asking a teacher or a peer for help or seeking out opportunities to practise using the language with others.
- *Affective:* Involves creating positive emotions during the task and staying motivated.

However, it is increasingly recognised that a single strategy is not, in itself, inherently cognitive, metacognitive, social or affective, but can have multiple functions, depending on how it is being used. For example, as suggested by Cohen and Wang (2018), the strategy of checking the meaning of a word with a more knowledgeable speaker could take on a metacognitive function (at the moment when learners are planning to implement this strategy), a social function (while engaging in the interaction) and a cognitive function (in processing the speaker's explanation). This example also illustrates that strategies are frequently used in sequences and clusters, rather than in isolation.

Why do strategies matter?

There is a growing body of evidence that suggests not only that there is a positive relationship between strategy use and attainment in language learning, but also that strategies are both 'teachable' and 'learnable'. Plonsky (2011), for example, conducted a meta-analysis of 61 studies into language learning strategy instruction across a range of contexts and detected a small to medium overall effect of strategy instruction. However, this was influenced by a range of factors. For example, effects were greater in studies in second language (rather than foreign language) settings and in some skill areas (such as speaking and reading) compared with others (such as writing). Yet, a more recent meta-analysis conducted by Ardasheva et al. (2017) found medium to large overall effects, which were almost two times larger than those reported in the above-mentioned 2011 study. The authors note that this increased effectiveness of strategy instruction may be due to a greater understanding of how to design and carry out programmes of strategy instruction, and also to a greater emphasis of more recent interventions on the metacognitive component. This highlights the importance of encouraging students to explicitly reflect not only on *what* they are doing in the classroom, but also on *how* they are doing it.

How do I use strategies in my teaching?

There are several general considerations which should be taken into account before designing and implementing a programme of language learning strategy instruction (LLSI):

- While strategies can be taught to learners at all levels, it is important to take into account their current level of proficiency when deciding which strategies to teach and whether to conduct the LLSI in the target language or in the students' first language (if shared with the teacher).
- As noted above, strategies can be taught across a range of skill areas; however, it is often advisable to begin by focusing on one particular skill area and then to gradually extend the range of strategies over time, so that students are not overwhelmed.
- LLSI should be integrated closely with regular instruction and normal classroom tasks, in order to highlight the relevance and application of strategies to the language learning process.
- LLSI should be made explicit, as raising students' awareness of their own strategy use is an important part of developing their wider strategic competence. Explicit instruction is also important for encouraging students to transfer strategies learned to other tasks and contexts.

There are various models of language learning strategy instruction; however, they all share similar steps, as shown in Figure 7.1:

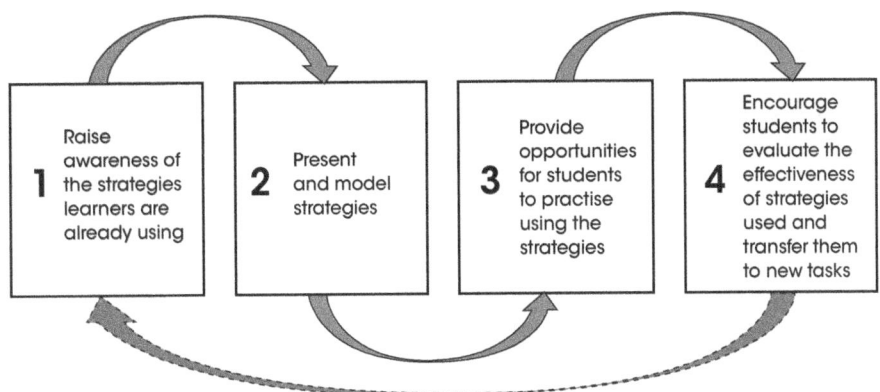

Figure 7.1: Stages of language learning strategy instruction (Forbes, 2020: 78)

- *Step 1* is important in raising awareness about the strategies that learners, and indeed their peers, are already using. This can be done through whole-class reflection and discussion immediately following the completion of a task.
- In *Step 2* the teacher then presents, models and explains the strategies, often through 'thinking aloud', in order to make explicit the internal processes that often go unnoticed. Strategies may be given names or acronyms to make them more memorable for students. The goal here is not for teachers to impose the 'right' strategies on learners, but instead to provide them with a range of strategies and the skills to be able to assess those which are most effective for them.
- *Step 3* typically takes the longest, and provides students with the time and opportunities to gain sufficient practice in using the strategies. Teachers typically begin by providing a scaffold to guide students, which is then gradually removed to allow for more independent practice and experimentation.
- *Step 4* is important for encouraging students to evaluate the effectiveness of their strategy use and to take ownership of their learning. This can be aided by providing students with feedback, not only on the final product but also on their process.

It is important to bear in mind that the above steps are not necessarily linear but should be considered as recursive, so that teachers and learners have the option of revisiting previous steps as needed. While designing and implementing effective strategy instruction can take time, evidence suggests that it can be beneficial for language learners.

Reflection

1. What strategies are my students already using? To what extent are they / am I aware of *how* they complete tasks (whether successfully or unsuccessfully)?

2. What opportunities are there to incorporate a reflection on strategies and language learning processes into my teaching?

3. Are there any particular skill areas my students are struggling with? Could strategies help them to overcome these challenges?

References

Ardasheva, Y., Wang, Z., Adesope, O. O., & Valentine, J. C. (2017). Exploring effectiveness and moderators of language learning strategy instruction on second language and self-regulated learning outcomes. *Review of Educational Research,* 87(3), 544–582. https://doi.org/10.3102/0034654316689135

Cohen, A. D., & Wang, I. K. H. (2018). Fluctuation in the functions of language learner strategies. *System,* 74, 169–182. https://doi.org/10.1016/j.system.2018.03.011

Forbes, K. (2020). *Cross-Linguistic Transfer of Writing Strategies: Interactions Between Foreign Language and First Language Classrooms.* Bristol: Multilingual Matters.

Griffiths, C. (2018). *The Strategy Factor in Successful Language Learning: The Tornado Effect* (2nd edition). Bristol: Multilingual Matters.

Plonsky, L. (2011). The effectiveness of second language strategy instruction: A meta-analysis. *Language Learning,* 61(4), 993–1038. https://doi.org/10.1111/j.1467-9922.2011.00663.x

Section 3: Beyond language skills – creativity and critical thinking

8 Critical thinking in the pandemic – the case of an Indonesian EFL classroom going online

Kate Wilson, Maya Defianty and Dadan

Critical thinking in language teaching

How do we harness the power of critical thinking in English language teaching (ELT)? This is a burning question, especially in countries where education authorities have set critical thinking as a key learning objective. In Indonesia, for example, teachers in all school disciplines are expected to promote critical thinking as a 21st-century skill, and to both teach and assess higher-order thinking skills (HOTS). For teachers of science, social studies or history, critical thinking may seem to be a natural fit, but ELT teachers may be somewhat bemused about how to integrate HOTS into their teaching.

Perhaps the best-known and most easily applicable categorisation of thinking skills is Bloom's taxonomy of learning objectives. The revised version of the taxonomy is described in Krathwohl (2002), and has been presented diagrammatically in countless forms, including Wilson (2019). The revised taxonomy presents a hierarchy of thinking skills: from the most basic skills of remembering and understanding, to higher-order skills of applying, analysing, evaluating and, at the apex, creating. These thinking skills can all be applied in language learning from two perspectives: firstly, thinking *about* the language itself, how it works and how to apply it in making meaning; and secondly, thinking *through* the language about the content that the language is expressing. In other words, from one perspective we can use critical thinking in learning about language forms and meanings and how to use them. From another perspective, we can use our emergent language skills to mediate critical thinking about all manner of topics and content. So there is plenty of scope for critical thinking in ELT classes.

In Figure 8.1, we have tried to capture how critical thinking applies in thinking *about* the language. Critical language learners do not simply 'parrot' the language, but take a delight in exploring how language is used to make meaning in different contexts. They use language to create texts of their own – spoken, written and multimedia texts of many kinds. Instead of didactically informing our students how language forms work, we can involve our learners themselves in analysing and evaluating how language is used in making meaning, and in applying language forms in a rich variety of contexts. By involving our learners in critical thinking activities, we can stimulate their interest in the language and their sense of ownership of the language. Critical thinking language learners tend to be engaged language learners.

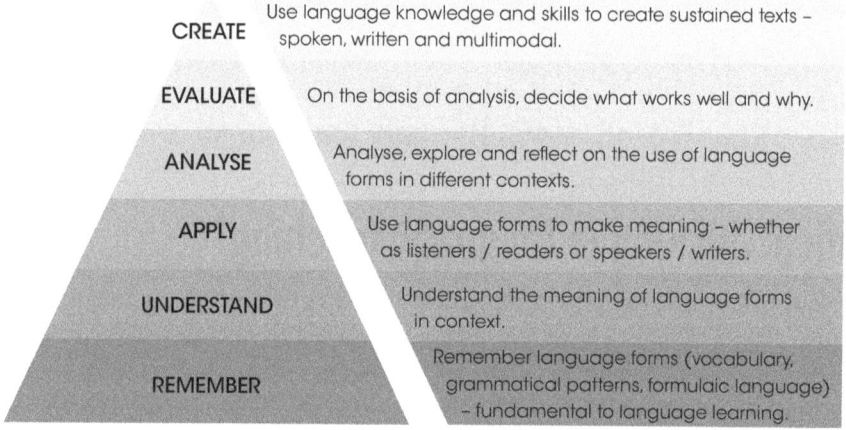

Figure 8.1: Applying Bloom's Taxonomy to language learning (derived from Krathwohl, 2002)

In this paper, we report on some of the findings from a research project conducted during the Covid-19 pandemic school lockdown in Indonesia, and we share two language learning tasks from our data which embodied good examples of critical thinking in ELT. We hope these exemplars will offer insights into how critical thinking can be applied in ELT, and encourage teachers in other ELT contexts to inject critical thinking into their teaching.

The research project

When the coronavirus pandemic hit in early 2020, teachers across the world were suddenly asked to teach remotely by whatever means they could. This was a huge challenge, especially in countries where technology was not already widely used in education, and where school children did not have ready access to computers.

In Indonesia, mobile phones are common, and smartphone usage is relatively widespread, but the cost of accessing the internet may still be prohibitive, and internet coverage is sometimes unreliable. It was in this context that we launched a research project to learn more about how high school English teachers in Indonesia were coping with the challenge of remote teaching. We called for volunteers via a WhatsApp professional development community, and ten teachers answered our call. Using Zoom, we interviewed these teachers in two focus groups of five teachers, and also individually. We also called for examples of lesson plans and students' work. The outcomes of the project are reported in greater detail in Defianty et al.

(2022). In particular, we asked teachers how they integrated communicative language learning into their online teaching.

Here we want to talk about how one outstanding teacher, pseudonym Daisy, integrated critical thinking into her teaching of communicative language skills in a Year 11/12 English class.

Daisy and her class

Daisy taught in a state high school in a reasonably affluent provincial capital in Indonesia. Although they were not generally from well-to-do families, most of the class had access to devices so they could use the internet and attend synchronous classes online (via WhatsApp or Zoom). There were 15–30 students in each class, and Daisy taught 11 classes in total. During the pandemic, Daisy's synchronous classes were well-attended, but the sessions were shorter than normal classroom hours, so the students were expected to do more individual work outside these class hours.

Daisy struck us as an enthusiastic and passionate teacher, strongly dedicated to her students, and keen to use technology in innovative ways. She believed that her students should become good citizens of the world; as she said, 'So it means that they need to have good action to help government, to help family and to help people who need their help'. It seemed that Daisy's success in getting the students to think critically was allied to her dedication to her students, her rapport with them, and the supportive community she had nurtured in her classes.

We were particularly impressed by two examples provided by Daisy, which demonstrated how she activated critical thinking in her ELT classes during the pandemic.

THE MILLENNIUM GOALS TASK

For this task, students were asked to make a one-minute speech about sustainable development. Each student had to choose one of the eight United Nations Millennium Development Goals, such as: 'Goal 1: Eradicate extreme poverty and hunger'. (See https://www.un.org/millenniumgoals/.)

After an introductory online session (synchronous) to engage the students' interest and explain the task, the students individually used the internet to research their chosen goal, to learn whether and where the goal had been reached, and what still remained to be done. They then had to compose their speech in written form, and share it with a friend for peer assessment.

Next, the students were instructed to learn and practise their speech. They were given several days to do this. Importantly, the students were required to end their speech with some ideas about how they, as individuals, could contribute to achieving the goal.

The students delivered their speeches in recorded break-out groups of eight (each student presented a different goal), and the final outcome was posted on Daisy's YouTube channel for other groups to view.

Finally, the class came together for a synchronous discussion online.

Daisy provided this example in response to our questions about how she had been able to promote communicative language skills in the online environment during the period of remote teaching. It is, indeed, an excellent example of how all four macroskills (listening, speaking, reading, writing) can be integrated in task-based learning. There was plenty of scope for valuable language learning in this task through both rich, authentic input and 'pushed output' (Swain, 2005). However, it is also a good example of how students can be encouraged to use critical thinking in language learning tasks. Table 8.1 summarises the critical thinking that was entailed at each stage of the task sequence in terms of thinking *about* the language and how it is used, and also *through* the language about the real-world content.

TASK SEQUENCE	CRITICAL THINKING *ABOUT* LANGUAGE	CRITICAL THINKING *THROUGH* LANGUAGE
Engage the students' interest	**Apply** language knowledge and skills in discussion	**Understand** the Millennium Goals
Research one of the Millennium Goals	**Apply** language knowledge and skills to read	**Understand** the Millennium Goals **Apply:** identify examples **Evaluate / Analyse** what is working and why
Write a paragraph	**Apply** language knowledge and skills to write **Create** a paragraph	**Summarise** key points **Apply:** exemplify successes **Analyse:** identify problems
Propose individual action	**Apply** language knowledge and skills	**Apply** new knowledge **Analyse:** propose solutions **Create** new ideas
Peer assess each other's writing	**Evaluate** peer paragraphs **Analyse** what works well and why	**Understand** the Millennium Goals
Learn by heart	**Remember**	
Present	**Remember / Apply**	**Understand** the Millennium Goals
Discuss	**Create:** use language knowledge and skills to express ideas and opinions	**Compare** success achieved in meeting various Millennium Goals **Compare** levels of success across countries / across provinces in Indonesia **Analyse** why some goals are achieved more successfully than others **Evaluate** students' proposed action

Table 8.1: A summary of the critical thinking opportunities at each stage of the Millennium Goals Task

There are some important points to note about the Millennium Goals Task:

- Peer assessment can be performed in a perfunctory way if students do not take it seriously. To ensure that peer assessment is truly productive and to maximise the potential for critical thinking about their own and others' writing, it can be helpful to involve students in co-designing a rubric. Several studies have shown that rubric training is essential in peer assessment (Li et al., 2020), and co-designing the rubric can help to deepen students' critical engagement with the task. The rubric can include both thinking *about* the language (language use) and thinking *through* the language (critical thinking about content). Productive peer assessment needs to become part of the culture of learning, so that students get used to participating responsibly in this important part of the task sequence.

- In this sort of task, it may be tempting for students to copy verbatim from websites. This may potentially negate the opportunity for critical thinking. So, factors have to be built into the task to ensure this doesn't happen. For example, a rubric for peer assessment can be designed to include a criterion, such as, 'expressed in the student's own words'.

- The students were instructed to propose individual actions to contribute to the achievement of the Millennium Goals. This was crucial in getting students to relate to, and engage with, the source material: to make meaning – as individuals – from the sources they accessed (Mickan, 2020). It was also an important factor in making sure that the final group discussion became dynamic and engaging.

- Daisy's choice of topic – the UN Millennium Goals – was an important topic for these Year 11/12 students, as the goals are the basis for social planning and development in Indonesia, as in many other countries. These students will soon be voting in regional and national elections.

 THE BOOK REVIEW TASK

In this task, students were asked to make a vodcast recording of a book review. Daisy introduced the book to her class; it was a short romance featuring young people like themselves. She read sections with the students and then had the students read the book individually. In the online synchronous class, they discussed the book in terms of how they perceived its strengths and weaknesses. They also read the review of another book, deconstructing the discourse of the review to analyse the stages of the genre, the interpersonal register, and the formulaic language that they could use in their own review.

The students individually made a list of their personal reasons for liking / not liking the assigned book. They then drafted their reviews, and rehearsed and peer reviewed each other's draft vodcasts.

The final vodcasts were uploaded on Daisy's YouTube channel. The energy and engagement apparent in the students' vodcasts was impressive.

As with the Millennium Goals Task, this task provided rich opportunities for communicative language learning, both through input and through output. There was also plenty of scope for recycling language, rehearsing, practising and remembering new language. Once again, an indispensable element of formative feedback was built into the task. In this task, the feedback was on the spoken presentation rather than the written draft, giving opportunities for feedback on pronunciation and fluency, rather than focusing on accuracy. And once again, the task afforded plenty of opportunities for critical thinking, as shown in Table 8.2.

TASK SEQUENCE	CRITICAL THINKING *ABOUT* LANGUAGE	CRITICAL THINKING *THROUGH* LANGUAGE
Engage the students' interest	**Apply** language knowledge and skills	**Reflect** on typical problems faced by teenagers like them
Read the book	**Apply** language knowledge and skills	**Understand** the author's meanings **Apply:** relate to own experience
Deconstruct model book review	**Analyse** the discourse of the book review genre: its stages, interpersonal register and language forms **Evaluate** what works well and why	**Understand** the book review genre
Discuss (in class) the strengths and weaknesses of the book	**Apply** language knowledge and skills **Analyse** and **evaluate** language used in the book	**Relate** the book to personal experience and social realities **Analyse** strengths and weaknesses **Evaluate**
Create draft vodcast	**Apply** language knowledge and skills	**Apply** and **evaluate** multimedia presentation techniques
Peer review	**Evaluate** language use **Analyse** what works and why	**Evaluate** content and presentation
Create and publish final product	**Create** polished vodcast	**Create** polished vodcast

Table 8.2: A summary of the critical thinking opportunities at each stage of the Book Review Task

Importantly, Daisy had built in scaffolding for this task (Hammond and Gibbons, 2005). Deconstructing the model review meant that the students were exposed to the language of the genre, but also, importantly, to the thinking routine embodied in the review genre:

- summarise
- present the strengths
- present the weaknesses
- draw a conclusion.

Such thinking routines are a valuable support in extending students' ability to think critically (see Harvard University's Project Zero – http://www.pz.harvard.edu/thinking-routines – for a full explanation of thinking routines (2016)).

Important points to note about the Book Review Task:

- The book that Daisy selected for her students to review related directly to their life experience. Critical thinking skills can be enhanced by igniting students' personal involvement.
- In this case, the book was selected by the teacher. A further level of personal engagement could have been added if students had chosen their own texts to review.
- The vodcast task stimulated the students' creativity and engagement. They went to considerable lengths to make their vodcasts lively by introducing images, animations, gesture and voice dynamics.
- Daisy provided plenty of scaffolding for this challenging task, making sure that the students were all able to succeed by engaging their interest, building up their linguistic resources and guiding them along the way (Hammond and Gibbons, 2005).

In this paper, we have tried to show that critical thinking can permeate language learning, particularly task-based language learning. Students may need to be encouraged, even pushed, to participate in critical thinking, especially if they are not accustomed to practising higher-order thinking skills. But through carefully structured task design, English language classes can be a rich breeding ground for future critical thinkers.

Reflection

1. Think about a task that you use in your own classroom. How can you maximise the potential for critical thinking?
2. Although Daisy had nearly 300 students altogether across her 11 classes, she was able to apply formative feedback through the implementation of peer assessment. She could also have used the task for summative assessment. What criteria to assess critical thinking could be developed for summative purposes, perhaps derived from Tables 8.1 and 8.2?

3. Daisy's lesson was a task-based lesson for intermediate and upper-intermediate students. How can critical thinking, as shown in Figure 8.1, be applied with lower level classes?

4. The two tasks described in this paper were implemented during the period of remote teaching, but the same tasks could have been used in face-to-face teaching. Do you think there is a link between autonomous learning and critical thinking in language learning?

References

Defianty, M., Wilson, K., & Dadan (2022). Surviving ERT: How an online professional learning community empowered teachers during the Covid-19 school lockdown in Indonesia. In J. Chen (ed.), *Emergency Remote Teaching and Beyond: Voices From World Language Teachers and Researchers*. Cham, Switzerland: Springer.

Hammond, J., & Gibbons, P. (2005). Putting scaffolding to work: The contribution of scaffolding in articulating ESL education. *Prospect*, 20(1), 6–30.

Harvard University, Graduate School of Education. (2016). Project Zero's Thinking Routine Toolbox. [online]. Available at: http://www.pz.harvard.edu/thinking-routines

Krathwohl, D. R. (2002). A revision of Bloom's taxonomy: An overview. *Theory into Practice*, (41)4, 212–218. https://doi.org/10.1207/s15430421tip4104_2

Li, H., Xiong, Y., Hunter, C. V., Guo, X., & Tywoniw, R. (2020). Does peer assessment promote student learning? A meta-analysis. *Assessment & Evaluation in Higher Education*, (45)2, 193–211. https://doi.org/10.1080/02602938.2019.1620679

Mickan, P. (2020). Transformative curriculum design: Functional linguistics applied in text-based teaching. In P. Mickan and I. Wallace (eds.), *The Routledge Handbook of Language Education Curriculum Design* (193–202). New York: Routledge.

Swain, M. (2005). The output hypothesis: Theory and research. In E. Hinkel (ed.), *Handbook of Research in Second Language Teaching and Learning*. New York: Routledge.

United Nations (n.d.). *We Can End Poverty: Millenium Development Goals and Beyond 2015*. Available at: https://www.un.org/millenniumgoals/

Wilson, K. (2019). *Critical thinking in EAP: A brief guide for teachers*. Part of the Cambridge Papers in ELT series. [pdf]. Cambridge: Cambridge University Press. Available at: https://www.cambridge.org/elt/blog/wp-content/uploads/2019/06/Critical-Thinking-in-EAP-Wilson-White-paper-21-May-19.pdf

9 Creating classroom conditions for creativity
Linda Fisher

Introduction

Creativity is a desirable quality, purported to motivate students and provide them with more flexible skills, though somewhat like gravity, it's perhaps easier to recognise than to define.

Nevertheless, in an attempt to do this I recently asked some languages teachers to express what creativity means for them and, what's more, to do this creatively. Mirroring the reaction we might get from our students, one said this was her 'worst nightmare', though others relished the task and within a few minutes had written, drawn, modelled (including out of crisp packets) their ideas.

In the end, like most of the authors who consider creativity (e.g. Runco and Jaeger, 2012), the teachers agreed that there are a couple of key elements, the first being some form of *originality* and the second *appropriateness* or *usefulness*. The teachers also tended to agree with the writers that creativity might also involve risk-taking, open and flexible thinking, and maybe some playfulness.

Creativity in the classroom

When most people think of creativity in schools, they tend to think of student-generated creative *products* (stories and poems, paintings, musical performances, etc.). While languages learners might sometimes produce such outputs, smaller creative acts occur all the time as:

> '... language is creative by its very nature. We can express or communicate one idea in many different ways. Furthermore, every expressed or communicated idea can provoke many different reactions. Every single sentence, phrase or word we say or write is created in a unique moment of communication and can be recreated, reformulated, paraphrased or changed according to the goals of the speaker or writer.'
>
> (Stepanek, 2015: 98)

So, creativity is intrinsic to the languages classroom, but how do we help people to recognise this and to build on it?

Naturally enough, this starts with teachers – both what *they* do and what they ask their students to do. As a starting point, teachers might consider the environment of the classroom and ask themselves: is there generally a playful atmosphere here, which might stimulate creativity (Cook, 2000) and is it a place where learners feel safe to take risks? Teachers can increase learners' confidence around risk-taking by modelling it more explicitly themselves, saying things like, 'I was wondering how you could best learn this, so today I'm going to try something new with you and we'll see if it works'. This generates inclusivity and helps learners understand that there is rarely one correct way to reach goals or to communicate. It also keeps things fresh, insofar as teachers are *planning* for creativity by thinking about using a wide variety of language inputs, learning processes and student outputs (Maley, 2015).

Inputs can come from different genre and media (e.g. graffiti, vlogs, pictures) to stimulate talk, and from many different fields (e.g. philosophy, art, business, sport) and can be adapted to the class's interests. Students can make assessments about others' language choices (e.g. which of these translations do I prefer and why?) and tap into their emotions, a neglected aspect of language classrooms (e.g. how does this text make me feel and why?). Learners can also be encouraged to attend more explicitly to the creativity inherent in language learning, such as: risk-taking (e.g. how else could I express that?), imagination (e.g. how can I use humour here?), or identity (e.g. how does what I'm saying here reflect my personality?). This can be summed up in Tables 9.1 and 9.2:

	LEARNERS ASSESSING OTHERS' USE OF LANGUAGE	**LEARNERS AND THEIR EMOTIONS**
Example questions	How else could this be expressed? How do these translations differ? Which do I prefer? Why?	How does this text make me feel? Why?

Table 9.1: Learners reacting to text

	LEARNERS AND CREATIVE CHOICES	**LEARNERS USING IMAGINATION**	**LEARNERS AND THEIR IDENTITIES**
Example questions	How can I express that? What are the alternatives? How are they different?	Can I use humour here? How might it affect the reader / listener? How would I say this if I were talking to my grandmother / the leader of my country / etc.?	How does what I am saying reflect my personality?

Table 9.2: Learners producing language

Offering choices

Autonomy and identity are both central to creativity – we are all unique and like to express that. Key to this authenticity and independence is offering choices about the form of outputs (e.g. posters, role plays, poetry, stories, videos, blogs, rap) and in which language(s) they are produced and presented (e.g. do we allow translanguaging?).

An important thing to remember for outputs is that tasks that are too open and go too far beyond the level at which learners are working may prove unproductive and need some constraints (Maley, 2015). This can be achieved by offering some framing, for example:

- including particular language features
- thinking about how to expand sentences in an interesting way
- thinking about unusual language to use
- using questions as frames for paragraphs.

However, we need to remember that creativity will involve some 'messiness', just as language itself does (Jones, 2018).

Returning to gravity where we started, Einstein *may* once have said that 'creativity is intelligence having fun', and surely we all want a bit more of that in our languages classrooms and in our lives?

References

Cook, G. (2000). *Language Play, Language Learning*. Oxford: Oxford University Press.

Jones, R. H. (2018). Messy creativity. *Language Sciences*, 65, 82–86. https://doi.org/10.1016/j.langsci.2017.06.003

Maley, A. (2015). Overview: Creativity – the what, the why and the how. In A. Maley & N. Peachey (eds.), *Creativity in the English Language Classroom*. London: British Council. Available at: https://www.teachingenglish.org.uk/sites/teacheng/files/pub_F004_ELT_Creativity_FINAL_v2%20WEB.pdf

Runco, M. A., & Jaeger, G. J. (2012). The standard definition of creativity. *Creativity Research Journal*, 24(1), 92–96. https://doi.org/10.1080/10400419.2012.650092

Stepanek, L. (2015). A creative approach to language teaching: A way to recognise, encourage and appreciate students' contributions to language classes. In A. Maley & N. Peachey (eds.), *Creativity in the English Language Classroom*. London: British Council. Available at: https://www.teachingenglish.org.uk/sites/teacheng/files/pub_F004_ELT_Creativity_FINAL_v2%20WEB.pdf

10 Developing creativity in the ELT classroom
Allen Davenport

What is creativity?

Although there is no definitive list to fully clarify what comprises 21st-century skills, there has been an increasing sense of urgency to include their development into many lessons and courses across the curriculum. In nearly all attempts to identify what these skills do to help make someone 'future-ready', some form of creativity (or creative thinking, creative problem solving, etc.) is identified.

While most teachers would agree that there is a need for creativity in the classroom, there still seems to be a mystical apprehension towards its integration. As Burkill and Eaton (2011: 78) rightly point out, 'this is not surprising for many are not too sure about the exact nature of creativity and where imagination leaves off and creativity weighs in'.

The first step then, in demystifying creativity, is to clarify precisely what is meant when it is included as a life competency or 21st-century skill. While many fanciful definitions of creativity can be found, when looking to integrate it into a language programme, Weisberg's (2020) description of creativity, that it is both novel and produced intentionally (goal-driven), is a good starting point, as this definition opens up access to, and opportunities for, creativity to both our students and ourselves.

Creativity is not a natural talent or an ability only reserved for (and to be developed in) the gifted student. Creativity can be nurtured throughout a person's life. However, given the nature of creativity itself, it is difficult – if not impossible – to teach creativity explicitly and directly in the classroom (Root-Bernstein and Root-Bernstein, 2011). However, there are moves that a teacher can make to develop and grow creativity in their learners. Creativity development does not have to be formed through a time-consuming structured lesson in and of itself; rather, it can be treated more like the teaching of pronunciation, which many practitioners tend to think is best dealt with by being integrated into other lessons (Watkins, 2014).

While there are many models of creativity and creative teaching available, I think there are three that are particularly well-suited to guiding teachers in the language classroom.

CATs Framework

The first is Kim's CATs framework (Kim, 2017). While this model was originally developed to describe the conditions to achieve 'innovation', the framework provides teachers with a practical path to nurture creativity. Kim's three steps build upon one another and can be summarised as follows:

- Step 1: Climate.
- Step 2: Attitudes.
- Step 3: Thinking.

The idea of cultivating creative climates reminds the teacher that the environment of the classroom matters. The creative classroom must be a place where all ideas are valued, mistakes are cherished, and where wrong answers are transformed into correct ones, not just marked as incorrect. Developing a creative climate begins with choosing tasks that allow an appropriate level of challenge, ensuring that the right level of support is available but not smothering. It is from this environment that creative attitudes (of both the learners and the teachers) are born.

Kim identified 27 creative attitudes, which were organised into four 'S' categories: Sun, Storm, Soil and Space.

SUN ATTITUDES	STORM ATTITUDES	SOIL ATTITUDES	SPACE ATTITUDES
Optimistic	Independent	Open-minded	Emotional
Big-picture thinking	Self-disciplined	Bicultural	Compassionate
Curious	Diligent	Mentored	Self-reflective
Spontaneous	Self-efficacious	Complexity-seeking	Autonomous
Playful	Resilient	Resourceful	Daydreaming
Energetic	Risk-taking		Nonconforming
	Persistent		Gender-bias-free
	Uncertainty-accepting		Defiant

Table 10.1: Kim's 27 creative attitudes (adapted from Kim, 2017)

Kim points out that nobody possesses all these attitudes but, in the proper creative climate, each of these attitudes can be developed through practice, which in turn enables a person's creative thinking skills. In this model these include: 'inbox thinking' (narrow and deep); 'outbox thinking' (quick and broad); and 'newbox thinking' (which connects and synthesises the two other types of thinking and transforms the idea into something novel). While perhaps oversimplifying Kim's model, it serves as a good reminder for teachers wishing to develop creativity in the classroom – a reminder that that the creative thinking which teachers desire in their learners results from learners' attitudes, which themselves are influenced by the environment.

William's Taxonomy

A second framework that is useful for language teachers is part of a model that was originally developed for gifted students, but which I think can be applied wholly across the curriculum. It is 'Dimension 3' of what is often referred to as 'William's Taxonomy' or the 'William's Model' (Davenport, 2017). While other dimensions of this model explicitly espouse teaching strategies, it is the explanation of student cognitive and affective behaviours that can be of particular use to teachers. The eight behaviours Williams identified can be separated into two strands, the cognitive (thinking) strand and affective (feeling) strand:

COGNITIVE BEHAVIOURS	AFFECTIVE BEHAVIOURS
Fluency – generating ideas	**Curiosity** – asking questions and exploring
Flexibility – sorting and changing categories	**Risk taking** – overcoming fear and taking a chance
Originality – coming up with a unique thought	**Complexity** – finding or building order in chaos
Elaboration – adding on to or enhancing an idea	**Imagination** – visualising and fantasising

Table 10.2: Cognitive and affective behaviours that can be used to develop creativity in the classroom (adapted from Moseley et al., 2005)

Teachers can use these descriptions in several ways to develop creativity in the classroom, by using them to identify creative opportunities in a coursebook, to formulate feedback on creativity students displayed during an activity, or to develop language tasks that incorporate one or more of these behaviours (Davenport, 2017).

Cambridge Life Competencies Framework

A third framework that is useful for teachers was developed specifically for language teachers as part of the larger *Cambridge Life Competencies Framework* (Cambridge University Press, 2020). In this framework, creative thinking is divided into three core areas:

- *Preparing for creativity* – which involves participating in activities that develop creative skills and looking at problems from different perspectives.
- *Generating ideas* – which involves basically the same cognitive behaviours (fluency, flexibility, originality and elaboration) from William's taxonomy.
- *Implementing ideas and solving problems* – which involve testing and revising ideas and being able to present and explain ideas to others.

The 'Cambridge Life Competency' of creative thinking is further broken down into components which can be used to develop 'can-do' statements. By pinpointing an aspect of creative thinking to the granular level, teachers can identify and develop creative outcomes in the classroom and focus on the functional language that students may need in order to facilitate the creative process.

Perhaps the most useful aspect to the *Cambridge Life Competencies Framework* is that it acknowledges that creative thinking develops over time, and that the expectations of creative thinking that a teacher would expect from a pre-primary student should not be the same as they would expect from an adult student. The framework allows for these variations by providing examples of 'can-do' statements and showing how they may change throughout a learner's journey. For example, one component of generating ideas – elaborating on and combining ideas – may be realised at different stages in the following way:

LEARNING STAGE	EXAMPLE 'CAN-DO' STATEMENT	EXAMPLE LANGUAGE
Pre-primary	Adds some details to their ideas	And then …
Primary	Finds new uses for objects and explains these ideas in detail	We can throw / drink / sit on it.
Secondary	Builds on others' ideas	I really like that idea. We could even …
Higher education	Brings in prior knowledge, perhaps from other subjects or contexts, to solve problems	This reminds me of …
At work	Brings in ideas and solutions from other life domains (e.g. social life, prior jobs, or hobbies) to help understand or solve current work challenges	Something that has worked for me before is …

Table 10.3: Examples of how creative thinking skills may develop throughout a learner's journey (adapted from Cambridge University Press, 2020)

Summing up

In summary, these three frameworks complement each other. Teachers who are familiar with them can start to shine a light through the fog that clouds the understanding of creativity and use them as practical guidance to facilitate the climate, attitude and behaviours – at the appropriate level of readiness – leading to the development of creativity in the language classroom.

Reflection

1. How should a teacher deal with mistakes in a classroom? How does this lead to a climate of creativity?
2. Look back at Kim's list of creative attitudes and choose one. What are some ways that a teacher could encourage that attitude in the classroom?
3. Think of a previous lesson you have taught. Can you identify any activities in that lesson that utilised one of William's identified cognitive or affective behaviours?
4. What is the relationship between components of creative thinking, 'can-do' statements, and example language?

References

Burkill, B., & Eaton, R. (2011). *Developing Teaching and Learning: The Textbook for the Cambridge International Certificate for Teachers and Trainers*. Cambridge: Cambridge University Press.

Cambridge University Press (2020). *The Cambridge Life Competencies Framework: Creative Thinking*. Cambridge: Cambridge University Press. Available at: https://issuu.com/cambridgeupelt/docs/cambridgelifecompetencies_creativethinkingbooklet_

Davenport, A. (2017). Appropriating a taxonomy of creativity for use in ELT. *Modern English Teacher*, 26(4), 8–11.

Kim, K. H. (2017). The Torrance tests of creative thinking – figural or verbal: Which one should we use? *Creativity. Theories – Research – Applications*, 4(2), 302–321. https://doi.org/10.1515/ctra-2017-0015

Moseley, D., Baumfield, V., Elliott, J., Higgins, S., Miller, J., Newton, D. P., & Gregson, M. (2005). *Frameworks for Thinking: A Handbook for Teaching and Learning*. Cambridge: Cambridge University Press.

Root-Bernstein, M., & Root-Bernstein, R. (2011). Can creativity be taught? *Psychology Today*. Available at: https://www.psychologytoday.com/us/blog/imagine/201104/can-creativity-be-taught

Watkins, P. (2014). *Learning to Teach English* (2nd edition). Peaslake: Delta Publishing.

Weisberg, R. (2020). Creativity: What it is. In *Rethinking Creativity: Inside-the-Box Thinking as the Basis for Innovation* (41–72). Cambridge: Cambridge University Press. https://doi.org/10.1017/9781108785259.002

Section 4: Data and technology

11 Making sense of big (and not so big) data with language learning analytics
Hayo Reinders

Introduction

The term 'big data' is used increasingly widely in many areas of life, from the health sciences to politics to social media. However, many teachers will understandably wonder what relevance big data has in language teaching and research. Surely the 20 or 30 learners in a class do not generate enough activity to warrant extensive analysis of the sort that requires endless server farms and complex applied mathematical techniques? And even if it did, surely this falls well outside of a teacher's responsibilities?

In this article, I will show that most teachers do, in fact, have much more data available to them than they realise, and data of the sort that can be easily accessed and used to improve learning outcomes using learning analytics. In other cases, fruitful collaborations with instructional designers and researchers can have a significant impact. In yet other cases, although the data and analyses may not involve teachers directly, the results can certainly have immediate pedagogical applications. I use a number of illustrations from studies in and beyond language classrooms to show how big (and not so big) data has been used in practice.

Some terminology

The term 'big data' has emerged in recent years to refer to the massive data sets generated by the likes of Google and Facebook. However, it has also taken on a more everyday meaning to describe the increasing amount of data generated in a range of domains, including education. Examples include: enrolment data, attendance records, academic indicators, such as progression figures and exam results, and numerous others.

Learning analytics and educational data mining (which we consider together here) are the processes used to make sense of such data (Gašević et al., 2017), or to put it another way, to turn data into information.

I like to think of information as data that is relevant to a particular person in a particular situation. Whereas medical health records are useful to a GP, I would not be able to understand or make use of them, and whereas a stack of exam papers is useful to me to understand how my learners are doing, they wouldn't be of interest to you and your students.

In an earlier article, I made a distinction between synchronous and asynchronous analytics (Reinders, 2018). Asynchronous analytics is the use of data to plan for future teaching or to reflect on past teaching, whereas synchronous analytics involves the use of data *during* a class to make in-the-moment decisions. An example of asynchronous data is the use of course registrations to identify the backgrounds and prior experience of learners so as to better prepare the course materials. An example of synchronous data is the use of chat window comments and polls to check comprehension. In principle, such data can be of any form; attendance records can be paper-based and questions are of course most commonly responded to by raising one's hand and speaking. The difference is that electronic data are far more numerous and have a number of advantages when it comes to storing, analysing and responding to them, which I will illustrate below.

Another distinction is the use that is made of the data. Truancy records are mostly used for administrative and compliance purposes (where schools have to report numbers to the local government, for example), whereas performance on a mid-term assignment is primarily of pedagogical use. The two are clearly interconnected, but in this article we will focus mostly on data that is of everyday value for teaching and learning.

Sources of data

Institutions collect a tremendous amount of data about learners: their prior educational experience, their GPAs, ethnicity, gender and so on, as well as performance indicators for the school, such as enrolments, drop-out rates and the like. Such data is usually available to individual teachers but may not always appear to be of immediate practical use. However, below we will look at ways in which such data can be used for the purposes of early identification of learning problems, the response to which will certainly involve the teaching staff.

Individual teachers have a range of additional data sources. One of these is the Learning Management System (LMS), the online learning environment through which teachers can post additional material, set homework tasks and collect assignments. Many teachers use the LMS for mostly administrative purposes, such as assigning homework or collecting assignments, but most programs have 'dashboards' that show detailed records, for example, the number of times students logged on and for how long, what percentage of online activities they completed successfully, how many forum posts they made, and so on.

Many commercial language learning resources used by schools record their own such data, which can usually easily be viewed or downloaded for further analysis. For example, the gradebook function in the Cambridge Learning Management System gives easy access to both the progress of the group as a whole and the activities that individuals are engaging with, and their success with those activities. And then there are the resources teachers use in class (either face-to-face or online): Kahoot, ClassDojo, Chaoxin, Socrative, and Seesaw are just some of the hundreds of popular programs used for learning activities, classroom communication, posting questions, and so on. Many of these allow teachers to elicit and reward students for certain types of behaviour, such as collaboration and negotiation, creativity, or constructive classroom demeanour.

Interactive whiteboards can store the content covered in class, online language tests can easily be marked and analysed, Zoom classes can store (and automatically transcribe) audio and video recordings, and (learner and native speaker) corpora can give teachers insights into their own learners' language development as well as language in use.

Clearly, a wide range of data sources is open for teachers to draw on.

Examples of big data and analytics in practice

Next, we will look at illustrations of the use of educational data for enhancing learning and teaching and report on some of the research into its benefits and drawbacks. The examples are grouped according to the pedagogical purposes for which the data have been used.

Using corpora for data-driven learning of vocabulary

Corpora have been used for decades to investigate authentic language use in many different contexts (e.g. spoken language, written texts, discipline-specific language). However, despite the availability of free corpora and tools to query them, they are largely underused by language teachers. They are also not commonly used to support data-driven learning, in which learners investigate the language by themselves (Chambers, 2019). Several reasons for this have been identified, but an almost exclusive focus in corpus publications on tertiary learners of English means many teachers are unaware of their potential. This is a missed opportunity, as a recent meta-analysis of 64 studies by Boulton and Cobb (2017) showed that data-driven learning was effective ($d = .95$) in supporting second language learning.

As an example of its successful integration in a language course, Pérez-Paredes et al. (2019) created a mobile language learning app based on freely available natural language processing tools in order to improve the writing skills of learners of English, German or Spanish who were aiming at an A2 or B2 level of proficiency. The app included tools such as a text analyser, a vocabulary profiler, and a part-of-speech tagger, which were all integrated in a publicly available program called Lextutor.

The learners were encouraged and supported to work with these user-friendly tools to inquire into their own and native speaker language use. In follow-up questionnaires and interviews, students said they particularly liked the instant and personalised feedback this gave them and the fact that the app made access to these tools easy. Perhaps more importantly in the context of this chapter, however, is that even without the app, the tools learners were given access to are freely available to all. By showing them how to work with authentic language data, learners can support their self-directed learning. This lessens reliance on the teacher as the source of L2 knowledge and empowers learners to take greater control over their own learning.

Supporting lesson planning in a writing course

As mentioned above, many applications used in class record a great deal of data about learners' activities and progress. For example, Wen and Song (2021) used a brainstorming and sharing tool called 'GS', for the purposes of supporting collaborative writing in the learning of Chinese as a second language in Singapore. GS assists learners in generating ideas, both individually and collaboratively, and in reflecting on and then selecting and prioritising these ideas. The application was available to learners both in class and outside. The course taught students how to emphasise meaning over form in the early drafting stages, to use stories to guide their writing, and to move from selecting appropriate vocabulary to drafting paragraphs and finally to completing essays.

The authors designed a simple analytical module for teachers and researchers to capture and analyse students' actions using the application, such as posting, editing or reading others' posts. A large amount of logged data was converted to indicators and visualised to show whether students actively engaged in the learning activity. For example, whether and how often students edited their post was used as an indicator of their use of active reflection on the writing process. The research team and the main class teacher examined these indicators and discussed the data at the end of each lesson, and used the information to adjust future teaching, as necessary.

Measuring learner engagement to support real-time teacher decision-making

Although the above application allows teachers to make quick decisions about the rest of the course, an example of the real-time use of data in class is provided by Bonner et al. (2022). As in many foreign language settings in Japan, teachers report significant challenges in keeping learners engaged. It is therefore vital for teachers to be able to identify when learners' engagement levels may be dropping and, over time, to establish what types of activities and content are most likely to be successful in raising and maintaining levels. Without analytics, most teachers have to rely on their impressions, which has obvious limitations. As Pei et al. (2017: 102) argue:

> 'Teachers, usually based on their experience, use their own gut feeling to translate student behavior and suspect if a student might drop out of a course or even abandon [their] studies ... But there is [a] low level of certainty in decisions that are based only on experience. Learning analytics has the capacity to add confidence to the decisions.'

To this end, the authors designed a small app called 'Classmoto' that teachers use to request learners to respond to three statements aimed to measure their cognitive, behavioural and emotional engagement levels using a slider (see Figure 11.1 below for the three prompts used). Once each student submits their feedback to the teacher, a red/yellow/green colour-coded display of all student responses appears on the teacher's screen, with red indicating a low level and green indicating a high level of reported agreement by a student (see the right-hand side of Figure 11.1). This allows teachers to see, at a glance, where the group is at and, if necessary, make adjustments. This also allows the data for an entire class to be reviewed and for longitudinal data, such as that recorded over an entire course, to be investigated and perhaps compared with either previous iterations of the course or those taught by other instructors. This enables teachers to establish what impact changes in, for example, materials used, course design or teaching method, have on learner engagement.

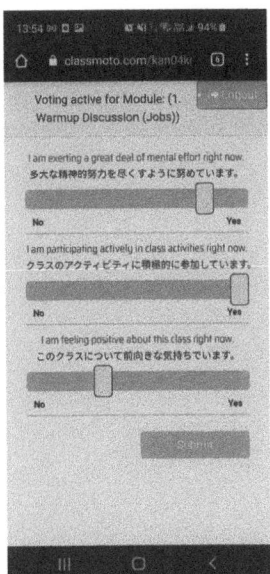 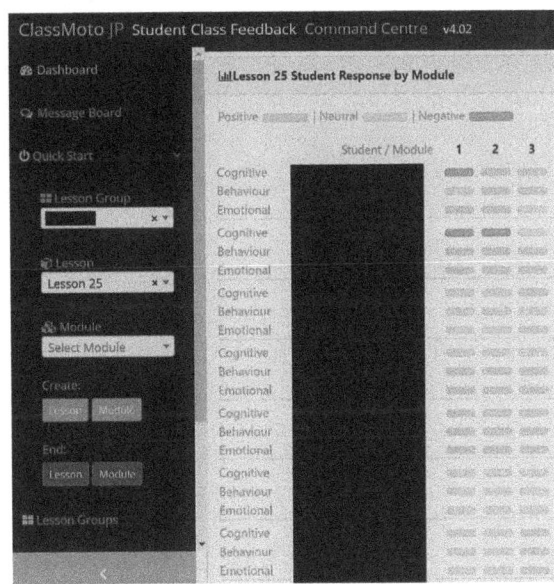

Figure 11.1: Classmoto student (left) and teacher (right) interface

Visualising French learners' progress online

The use of visualisations, such as shown in Figure 11.1, can provide quick feedback to teachers. An interesting example of this is reported by Youngs et al. (2018). This involved collaboration between a researcher and a team of instructors. In her study she helped teachers of French in the United States identify which course materials proved to be either too difficult for their learners or otherwise problematic. Specifically, she drew data from students' online activities to determine:

- which students completed which items
- which items students skipped or answered incorrectly on the first attempt
- which lesson items or sections students skipped completely.

This helped her to identify outliers, troubling patterns and odd trends in student responses, in order to identify vocabulary that was beyond the students' level. Given the large number of data points (one each for every student's response to every question in the course materials over an entire course), Youngs created a visualisation tool that created plots and collated basic statistics to show student performance by item and lesson in real time. As a result, teachers were able to quickly identify issues and respond to them immediately. Such 'dashboards' can also be provided to learners (see page 97 for a project that made a learning dashboard available to learners).

Using historical data to investigate course outcomes

An example of the use of student data is provided by Schulze and Scholz (2018). The authors retrieved student data from a period of ten years, to compare online and on-campus German language courses at the University of Waterloo in Canada. As both course types used the same textbook materials, syllabus and assessments, a direct comparison was possible. The authors conclude:

> *'Although many students prefer a language-learning experience in the classroom, including the face-to-face social interaction with the instructor and their peers, they welcome the online learning opportunity, particularly when classroom options prove difficult or are impossible. And most importantly, given equal student effort and engagement, student learning outcomes in metalinguistic and cultural knowledge and in written and oral language proficiency are at par after a term or two with those of on-campus courses.'*
>
> (Schulze and Scholz, 2018: 202)

What is relevant in the context of our discussion of learning analytics is that the data used for the study was readily available and similar data would likely be available to many teachers in other contexts. In this study, by drawing on historical data, a total of 6840 usable student course records were obtained, providing information about student enrolments, continuation or withdrawal and final grade. Because of the large amount of data, the results provide robust insights into students' learning.

Using a Learning Management System for optimising course design

As noted above, Learning Management Systems (LMS) or Virtual Learning Environments (VLE)[3] record a wealth of information. Rienties et al. (2018) used the data recorded by the Open University's VLE to investigate how module design decisions affected learner engagement of a total of 2111 learners of French and Spanish.

The authors looked at the average time spent on the VLE per week (in minutes) and the average time spent per session on the VLE, as well as information about the types of content, materials and tools (e.g. discussion forums, videoconferencing) learners used. They found that 55% of the variance in weekly engagement could be attributed to course design. The data could then be used to identify how to optimise the course content and activities for future iterations. For example, activities linked with either assessments or involving L2 production were shown to result in greater engagement.

Providing data to learners

VITAL (Visualisation Tools and Analytics to Monitor Online Language Learning and Teaching) was a two-year Erasmus+ project (2015–2017) funded by the European Commission (Thomas et al., 2017). One of its aims was to make learning data available not only to administrators but also to teachers, and – our focus here – learners. By providing a dashboard with visualised insights into their patterns of engagement and interaction, learners could better understand their own learning. One of the foci was to explore the difference between the workplans, or intended usage of the activities, and what the language students actually did when online. Research into learners' experiences of working with their own data offered some interesting insights and also pointed to the need for further research. For example, Chinese undergraduates commented that they would like to see the average grades of the group they belonged to, as this was a typical feature of student life in their own country. This was the minority view, however, and other students argued that being able to see this information on a day-to-day basis might increase anxiety and pressure to achieve group benchmarks, rather than compete against themselves and their own personal targets. Clearly, further investigation needs to be done in terms of what types of data are most useful for learners and how these are presented, but the fact that learners *can* get insight into their learning, if they choose, firmly increases their level of agency of their language learning.

---

3 In the literature, a distinction is made between these two but for the purposes of this article we will consider them together.

Investigating success in language MOOCs

Language MOOCs (Massive Open Online Courses) have been around for over a decade now and, at present, there are more than 400 language course MOOCs on offer globally (Class Central, 2021). Despite their popularity, a number of issues have emerged in practice, most importantly low participation and completion rates. Common reasons for this include the lack of opportunities for social interaction and the lack of personalisation, meaning that learners may not find the (level of) content they are looking for.

To overcome some of these issues, Jitpaisarnwattana et al. (2021) designed and implemented a presentation MOOC for working professionals in Thailand that included a range of features designed to allow participants to create their own learning pathway and to collaborate with others. They analysed how 270 learners in the MOOC made use of its different features and opportunities for learning, in order to identify the types of learning behaviour that were related to course completion. Binary logistic regression and feature extraction techniques demonstrated that, amongst others, working in groups and creating a learning plan were important factors associated with course completion, while interacting with other learners online was not – meaning that feeling part of a group increased learners' motivation to continue their learning, but the actual amount of interaction did not have an impact. This is an important insight, as it runs counter to previous research findings that did not distinguish between different types of interaction and would have been difficult to establish without the statistical modelling used in the analysis.

Language MOOCs are a good example of a learning environment that is inherently rich in data and tools for analysing learning behaviours. As more MOOCs and other forms of large online communities become commonplace, teachers can draw on learners' experiences in them to gain insight into their prior learning, preferences and particular challenges.

Potential benefits and drawbacks of using analytics

The above examples illustrate a number of potential benefits for the various types of data most teachers have access to. I will briefly highlight the main ones here.

Early intervention

By obtaining and analysing learner data as courses progress, it may be possible to identify students whose learning behaviours indicate they may be at risk. In the example of Classmoto above, students whose engagement scores are below the class average – or whose levels drop significantly as the course progresses – could be approached by the teacher to resolve any issues quickly, before they become major challenges.

Targetted support

Early intervention also means that support can be personalised and targetted at specific (groups of) students. For example, learners of French in the project by Youngs described above – who did not complete certain online activities, or took significantly more tries or time – could be offered supplementary support, while other learners would simply continue the planned course progression. This is in contrast to most traditional courses where a drop in, for example, average test scores for a cohort, results in the implementation of support measures (such as remedial classes) for all learners, which is both a drain on resources and an inefficient use of time for those students who do not need the additional support.

Predicting student performance

As more data becomes available (either within a school, for example, from multiple cohorts or different subjects, or between schools), it may become possible to identify correlations between certain learning behaviours and learning outcomes. This may lead to the identification of 'proxy measures'. For example, at the University of Maryland, it was observed that students who obtained low grades used the VLE 40% less than students who obtained higher grades. As usage of the VLE can be relatively easily recorded, it becomes possible to identify students who may be likely to underperform. This then allows the school to follow-up with these students to identify if they are having pedagogical or other difficulties (in some cases, lack of use of the VLE will simply be because of technical problems, such as not having received a password). Another advantage of proxy measures is that they can often be obtained much more quickly than traditional measures. In the example above, the University would normally have to wait until at least the end-of-term scores to be collected and analysed, but a reasonable measure of VLE use can be obtained within two or three weeks from the start of the academic year.

Identifying successful learning patterns

What makes some learners more successful than others? Learning analytics is starting to offer additional insights into this age-old question. For example, time-on-task (how much time learners spend studying the language) has long been recognised as a major predictor of success, but finer-grained analyses can show that time spent on certain types of tasks may be far more important than others, or that certain other conditions have to be met before learners can gain maximum benefit from their efforts. For example, Fang et al. (2019) used structural equation modeling to establish that (in the context of MOOCs) having an immersive experience and having one's needs met for autonomy, connectedness and competence are precursors to success.

Fostering learning agency

As mentioned above, providing access to individual learning data can help learners take increased responsibility for their own learning. This depends on a developing recognition that learners have a right to their own data (see below) and that teachers have the responsibility for empowering learners with the skills necessary to make sense of this data.

Obtaining comparative insights

At a larger scale, the insights from the data generated in multiple classrooms, schools or even districts, across multiple subjects and years, can yield tremendously powerful insights into which factors support or hinder improvement in learning outcomes. The field of language education is at the very early stages of this development but as more teaching is now carried out online – and as teachers have easier access to more data – it is likely that initiatives for sharing and analysing data across institutional boundaries will increase.

Despite these benefits, the use of learning analytics presents a number of significant risks. Beyond the widely recognised issues in the use of technology, such as unequal access, and privacy and security threats (see, for example, NMC, 2015), in the case of big data and analytics there are questions around the ownership of – and access to – learning data (Jones, 2019). As we have seen in some of the examples above, enabling learners to view and analyse their own learning is a powerful learning tool, but this does not clarify what happens to the data once learners leave a course or school. Will they be able to take the data with them? Will the school still have access to it? Will it be able to use or even sell that data? Clearly, these are all increasingly pressing questions as more data is collected.

More perniciously, there is a real danger in decisions being made on the basis of data that are incomplete, inaccurate, or that include an inherent bias. Groups of learners may be targeted on the basis of previous experiences or their backgrounds, thus predetermining them to certain learning pathways and possibly excluding them from others. And even if the data are accurate and comprehensive, there is a danger of over monitoring and micro-managing learners and losing sight of the individual in the learning process.

> *Gelan et al. (2018) speak of a developing 'wariness of systematic data logging if perceived as a control or surveillance mechanism rather than as a tool for greater pedagogical support'.*

Summing up

Clearly, as language educators and researchers we have a phenomenal resource available to us now. And as 'with great power comes great responsibility', a first step is for teachers and learners to become aware of the benefits and drawbacks of the new technology and to work together to establish how to best support improved learning outcomes for all. I hope the illustrations in this chapter offer a useful starting point.

Reflection

1. Does your institution have a Learning Management System? What data can you easily access from it? Do teachers have access to professional development so that they can make the most of the data?
2. If you have access to data derived from a course that you teach, what can you conclude from it?
3. What data would you most like to have about your learners, or your courses? How could you use that data?
4. How could such data be used to empower learners (for example, by providing them access to their own learning records)?
5. How will you deal with the ethical, security and privacy issues involved in collecting and analysing such data?

References

Bonner, E., Garvey, K., Miner, M., Godin, S., & Reinders, H. (2022). Measuring real-time learner engagement in the Japanese EFL classroom. *Innovation in Language Learning and Teaching*, 1–11. https://doi.org/10.1080/17501229.2021.2025379

Boulton, A., & Cobb, T. (2017). Corpus use in language learning: A meta-analysis. *Language Learning*, 67(2), 348–393.

Chambers, A. (2019). Towards the corpus revolution? Bridging the research–practice gap. *Language Teaching*, 52(4), 460–475. https://doi.org/10.1111/lang.12224

Class Central (2021). Available at: https://www.classcentral.com/subject/foreign-language

Fang, J., Tang, L., Yang, J., & Peng, M. (2019). Social interaction in MOOCs: The mediating effects of immersive experience and psychological needs satisfaction. *Telematics and Informatics*, 39, 75–91.

Gašević, D., Kovanović, V., & Joksimović, S. (2017). Piecing the learning analytics puzzle: A consolidated model of a field of research and practice. *Learning Research and Practice*, 3(1), 63–78.

Gelan, A., Fastré, G., Verjans, M., Martin, N., Janssenswillen, G., Creemers, M., Lieben, J., Depaire, B., & Thomas, M. (2018). Affordances and limitations of learning analytics for computer-assisted language learning: A case study of the VITAL project. *Computer Assisted Language Learning*, 31(3), 294–319.

Jitpaisarnwattana, N., Reinders, H., & Darasawang, P. (2021). Understanding the roles of personalization and social learning in a language MOOC through learning analytics. *Online Learning Journal*, 25(4), 324–343.

Jones, K. M. (2019). Learning analytics and higher education: A proposed model for establishing informed consent mechanisms to promote student privacy and autonomy. *International Journal of Educational Technology in Higher Education*, 16(1), 1–22.

NMC. (2015). *The NMC Horizon Report: 2015 Higher Education Edition*. Available at: http://www.nmc.org/publication/nmc-horizon-report-2015-higher-education-edition/

Pei, Z., Han, L., & Gu, J. Q. (2017). Application of big data in higher education for learning analytics. Proceedings of the 2017 3rd Conference on Education and Teaching in Colleges and Universities (CETCU, 2017), *Advances in Social Science, Education and Humanities Research*, 93, 100–104. Atlantis Press.

Pérez-Paredes, P., Guillamón, C. O., Van de Vyver, J., Meurice, A., Jiménez, P. A., Conole, G., & Hernández, P. S. (2019). Mobile data-driven language learning: Affordances and learners' perception. *System*, 84, 145–159.

Reinders, H. (2018). Learning analytics for language learning and teaching. *JALT CALL Journal*, 14(1), 77–86.

Rienties, B., Lewis, T., McFarlane, R., Nguyen, Q., & Toetenel, L. (2018). Analytics in online and offline language learning environments: The role of learning design to understand student online engagement. *Computer Assisted Language Learning*, 31(3), 273–293.

Schulze, M., & Scholz, K. (2018). Learning trajectories and the role of online courses in a language program. *Computer Assisted Language Learning*, 31(3), 185–205.

Thomas, M., Reinders, H., & Gelan, A. (2017). Social learning analytics in online language learning: Challenges and future directions. In L. L. Wong & K. Hyland (eds.), *Faces of English Education* (197–212). New York: Routledge.

Wen, Y., & Song, Y. (2021). Learning analytics for collaborative language learning in classrooms: From the holistic perspective of learning analytics, learning design and teacher inquiry. *Educational Technology & Society*, 24(1), 1–15.

Youngs, B. L., Prakash, A., & Nugent, R. (2018). Statistically-driven visualizations of student interactions with a French online course video. *Computer Assisted Language Learning*, 31(3), 206–225.

12 Digital pedagogy and language teaching and learning – from research to practice

Niall Curry

Introduction

While digital pedagogy is by no means a new endeavour, its role in language education – and education more generally – has grown considerably in recent years. Much of the most recent, accelerated growth can be attributed to the mass movement of education to online spaces during the Covid-19 pandemic. However, Covid-19 notwithstanding, arguably, the changing winds and shifting sands that have perennially shaped English language teaching practices (Marckwardt, 1972) were likely guiding educational technology and language education to continue to evolve together and shape one another (Carrier and Nye, 2017).

Critiques of digital pedagogies during the Covid-19 pandemic argue, quite rightly, that many organisations, teachers, and students were not prepared to make the transition to digital teaching and learning. As such, many practices in digital pedagogies at this time reflect a crisis-response to digital pedagogy that is not built upon established and research-informed educational practices (Adedoyin and Soykan, 2020). Therefore, it becomes important to disentangle crisis practices from research-informed practices and reflect upon how to best support and deliver impactful digital language pedagogies. To this end, this short chapter brings together different perspectives on teaching and learning a language with technology.

What is this chapter about?

This chapter aims to:

- highlight the synergetic relationship between pedagogy and technology
- point to guiding principles that can support effective practices in digital language pedagogy
- offer useful points for reflection to guide personalised teacher development in this area.

Teaching and learning language with technology: unpacking a complex relationship

Teaching and learning language with technology draws on research from many fields, such as data-driven learning (Pérez-Paredes, 2019), educational technology (Thorne and May, 2017) and (I)CALL – (intelligent) computer-aided language learning (Curry and Riordan, 2021). What transcends these various foci is a strong consideration of the relationship that exists between pedagogy and technology. That is to say, there is a consistent consideration of how teachers are guided to merge their pedagogical approaches with their technological practices.

In earlier work on blended language teaching, teachers are guided to use technology to replicate effective practices that occur in the analogue teaching world (McCarthy, 2016). Similarly, Selwyn (2011) calls for a deep consideration of the goodness of the fit between technology and pedagogy, arguing that technology will not automatically enhance language teaching and learning. Echoing such views, a typical argument encountered in discussions of digital pedagogy, and one I have made myself (Curry, 2018), is to 'put the pedagogy first'. Largely, this is well meaning and aims to support teachers by encouraging them to draw on their existing knowledge of language teaching and learning to inform their use of technology as they develop an awareness of what might be termed 'digital language pedagogy'. This perspective is well espoused in the literature (cf. Fox, 2003; Fullan, 2013) and largely serves to guide teachers to treat technology like any other resource, e.g. a coursebook.

In attempting to visualise this model of the relationship between technology and pedagogy, Figure 12.1 presents the teachers' knowledge as including their understanding of language pedagogy, which, in turn, contains within it a knowledge of using technology to facilitate language learning.

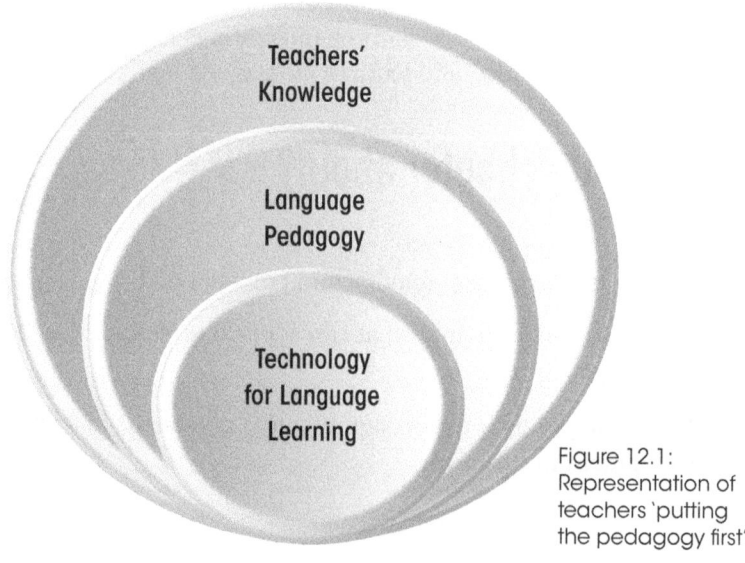

Figure 12.1: Representation of teachers 'putting the pedagogy first'

However, a recent paper by Tsui and Tavares (2021) problematises this widely held view, positing that one ought not to consider the relationship between pedagogy and technology as a dichotomous and unidirectional one. For them, such a view blurs the truly complex relationship between language pedagogy and technology, which they argue is synergetic, iterative and multidirectional in nature. In this way, pedagogy and technology can shape and be shaped by one another. It may seem obvious that technology should facilitate pedagogy; however, technology can also develop pedagogies by offering new ways of differentiating content, for example, where the speed of videos could be changed to slow down or speed up recordings in mixed-ability classrooms. Following this logic, the relationship between pedagogy and technology is one of co-construction, varying according to curricular, environmental and contextual stimuli, such as classroom constraints and learning objectives, as Figure 12.2 indicates.

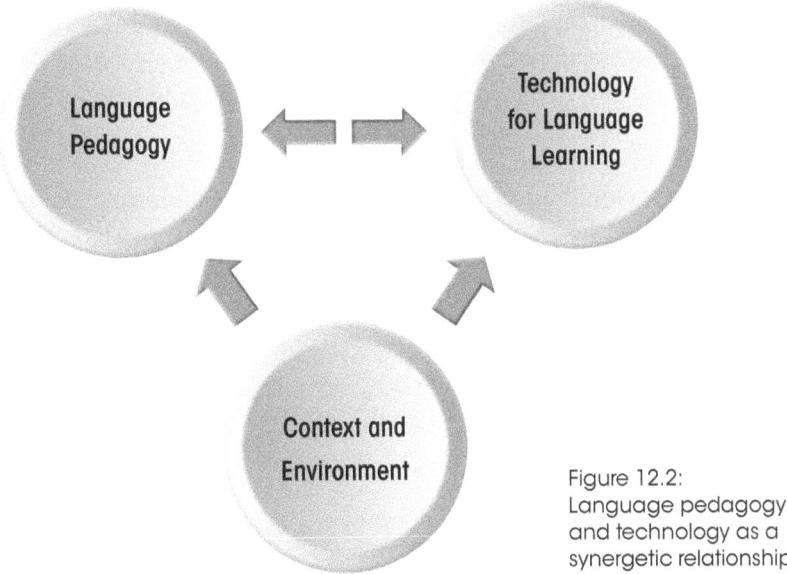

Figure 12.2: Language pedagogy and technology as a synergetic relationship

Of course, Tsui and Tavares (2021) recognise that a focus on pedagogy is of critical importance. However, they argue that the openness to allow technology to reframe and reimagine pedagogy is important, as this is one of language technology's key affordances. As such, to develop language teachers' practices, it may be more beneficial to accept that the relationship between pedagogy and technology is a complex one. In doing so, the multidirectional ways pedagogy and technology shape each other can be explored more deeply. With this discussion in mind, the following section offers guiding principles for developing an iterative approach to digital language pedagogy.

Towards an iterative digital language pedagogy

In developing a digital pedagogy, research offers a number of valuable guidelines. For example, research suggests that digital language learning ought to: engage and motivate learners (Gao and Ma, 2020); develop autonomous learners (Niinivaara and Vaattovaara, 2018); facilitate interactive, socialised and collaborative learning (Thorne et al., 2009); and create spaces for self-regulation and self-development (Matsuoka, 2014). However, to inform digital language teaching practically in this way, there is a need for local and contextualised efforts and commitment. Without the appropriate infrastructure and support, and depending on the student body, digital pedagogies remain inherently variable.

In developing an approach to digital pedagogy, consideration must be given to contexts, students and shared language learning aims. In working with technology, the goal to facilitate teaching and learning can be met by drawing on the field's collective expertise in language education. This is expertise that is also not static, but dynamic and ever-evolving. As such, keeping up-to-date with developments is an obstacle to be overcome. However, further challenges emerge. Not only is there a need to develop an awareness of current knowledge and practices in the field, there is also a need to develop them by continuing to innovate and experiment with technology and share experiences of doing so. In this way, working within the complex systems that govern language pedagogy and technology, new and innovative practices can emerge that fit well within a range of digital teaching contexts.

A localised and iterative digital pedagogy allows us to draw on macro themes in educational research and use them to guide teaching practices. For example, knowing that learners learn effectively in social contexts, one could argue that the use of social media and the internet can effectively realise pedagogical goals of facilitating authentic social engagement (Chapelle, 2003). Moreover, in letting technology guide pedagogy, using learner engagement data – such as that available in tools like Write & Improve (Curry and Riordan, 2021) – to inform teaching, can allow for the development of data-driven learning objectives. In such ways, one can develop a robust and reflexive approach to digital language pedagogies.

Closing remarks and points of reflection

In engaging in a brief discussion of digital pedagogy and language teaching and learning, this chapter aimed to draw attention to the challenges of developing digital pedagogies during a crisis, such as the Covid-19 pandemic, and the importance of disentangling crisis and digital pedagogies. Recognising the inherent value that research affords the informing of research-led digital pedagogies, the teaching and learning of language with technology was discussed.

This discussion centred on the complex relationship between technology and language learning and offered guidelines for the development of a digital pedagogy.

Though there are often efforts to systematise teaching and learning, it is not a science *per se*. Rather, it is an extremely variable practice that is universal and global, yet heavily and deeply localised. In engaging with research to inform digital language pedagogies (or any pedagogies for that matter), caution is required. There is a need to be cautious of depending too much on heavily localised research to inform practices in very different contexts, and of considering such research as irrelevant simply because it does not entirely reflect specific contexts. A more fruitful practice would be a critical one, which affords a deep engagement with research to foster experimental approaches that may lead to new, creative, and innovative practices. With this in mind, the following self-reflective guide offers a means to develop critical practices for digital pedagogies.

Reflections

Reflecting on digital pedagogy for language teaching and learning: Part 1

Use this first question to identify and understand your own practices in order to find a means to develop them.

1. Think back to your first experiences with digital pedagogy. How has your approach changed over time?

Reflecting on digital pedagogy for language teaching and learning: Part 2

Next, think about why the changes you identified have occurred.

2. To what extent do you 'put the technology first'? Or do you take a more synergetic view of language pedagogy and technology as shaping one another?

Reflecting on digital pedagogy for language teaching and learning: Part 3

Now, consider the following question to look forward and rationalise your decisions and practices.

3. How will you determine if the changes you make / do not make to your practices have a positive impact on your teaching?

Reflecting on digital pedagogy for language teaching and learning: Part 4

Finally, reflective practices are ongoing and we should not consider this the endpoint. Therefore, the final reflective question offers scope for sustained and future development.

4. Looking forward, how will you continue to develop your approach to digital pedagogies?

References

Adedoyin, O. B., & Soykan, E. (2020). Covid-19 pandemic and online learning: The challenges and opportunities. *Interactive Learning Environments*, 1–13.

Carrier, M., & Nye, A. (2017). Empowering teachers for the digital future: What do 21st-century teachers need? In M. Carrier, R. M. Damerow & K. M. Bailey (eds.), *Digital Language Learning And Teaching: Research, Theory, and Practice* (208–221). London: Routledge.

Chapelle, C. A. (2003). *English Language Learning and Technology*. Amsterdam: John Benjamins.

Curry, N. (2018). Putting the pedagogy first in digital pedagogies. *World of Better Learning*. Cambridge: Cambridge University Press. Available at: https://www.cambridge.org/elt/blog/2018/10/05/putting-the-pedagogy-first-in-digital-pedagogies/

Curry, N., & Riordan, E. (2021). Intelligent CALL systems for writing development: Investigating the use of Write & Improve for developing written language and writing skills. In K. B. Kelch, P. Byun, S. Safavi & S. Cervantes (eds.), *CALL Theory Applications for Online TESOL Education* (252–273). Hershey, PA: IGI Global.

Fox, R. (2003). Pedagogy first: Developing collaborative e-learning environments. Session 2: E-learning Interface for Multicultural Co-existence. *E-learning Beyond Cultural and Linguistic Barriers: Co-existence and Collaboration* (116–147). NIME 2002 INTERNATIONAL SYMPOSIUM. Available at: https://core.ac.uk/download/pdf/235176788.pdf

Fullan, M. (2013). *Stratosphere: Integrating Technology, Pedagogy, and Change Knowledge.* Don Mills, ON: Pearson.

Gao, J., & Ma, S. (2020). Instructor feedback on free writing and automated corrective feedback in drills: Intensity and efficacy. *Language Teaching Research*. https://doi.org/10.1177/1362168820915337

Marckwardt, A. (1972). Changing winds and shifting sands. *MST English Quarterly*, 21, 3–11.

Matsuoka, R. (2014). Socio-psychological analysis of digital employment among Japanese English learners. *Procedia – Social and Behavioral Sciences*, 136, 54–58.

McCarthy, M. (2016). Issues in second language acquisition in relation to blended learning. In M. McCarthy (ed.), *The Cambridge Guide to Blended Learning for Language Teaching* (7–16). Cambridge: Cambridge University Press.

Niinivaara, J., & Vaattovaara, J. (2018). Learners' and teachers' voices in developing digital language learning environments: Insights from a survey. *Language Learning in Higher Education*, 8(1), 133–156.

Pérez-Paredes, P. (2019). A systematic review of the uses and spread of corpora and data-driven learning in CALL research during 2011–2015. *Computer Assisted Language Learning*, 1–26.

Selwyn, N. (2011). Digitally distance learning: A study of international distance learners' (non)use of technology. *Distance Education*, 32(1), 85–99.

Thorne, S. L,. & May, S. (eds.) (2017). *Language, Education and Technology* (3rd edition). New York: Springer.

Thorne, S. L., Black, R. W., & Sykes, J. M. (2009). Second language use, socialization, and learning in internet interest communities and online gaming. *The Modern Language Journal*, 93, 802–821.

Tsui, A., & Tavares, N. J. (2021). The technology cart and the pedagogy horse in online teaching. *English Teaching & Learning*, 45(1), 109–118.

About the authors

Niall Curry is a lecturer and ASPiRE Fellow at Coventry University. His interdisciplinary research spans a range of areas in applied linguistics. These include a focus on corpus linguistics, contrastive linguistics, academic writing and metadiscourse in English, French and Spanish, language change, discourse analysis, and TESOL and language teaching materials development. Previously, Niall has worked in industry, at Cambridge University Press, and internationally, at universities in Ireland and France.

Dadan is a teacher at Bandung Independent School, where he teaches Bahasa Indonesia to non-Indonesian students. He has extensive experience in teaching English in several secondary schools in Bandung, Indonesia. He is currently involved in several projects concerning teacher professional development, and has published several book chapters on language pedagogy. His research includes ICT in English language learning.

Allen Davenport is the Professional Learning and Development Manager for the Southeast Asia (ASEAN) region at Cambridge University Press. He has been actively involved in education for more than two decades as a teacher, training consultant, academic director, and examiner for several international exam boards. Allen holds a bachelor's degree in foreign languages, literatures and linguistics and a master's degree in education, with a focus on academic counselling and student development. His professional interests include the development of creativity in learners, exploring and applying educational frameworks, and investigating how English language teaching is adapting to meet the changing needs of language learners.

Maya Defianty is a lecturer and a member of Center of Excellence at the University of UIN Syarif Hidayatullah, Jakarta. She has extensive experience in working with English teachers in Indonesia on how to enhance their teaching practice. Her research interest is on teachers' classroom assessment practice, critical thinking skills and teacher professional development.

Linda Fisher is Professor in Languages Education in the Faculty of Education, University of Cambridge, where she teaches on a number of second language and teacher education programmes. Her research focuses on multilingual identity, creativity, metaphor in relation to belief schemata, second language teacher education, motivation, and the academic and social integration of English as an Additional Language learners. She led on the Multilingual Identity in Language Learning research strand of the *Multilingualism: Empowering Individuals, Transforming Societies* project (AHRC, 2016–2020) and researched creativity in the languages classroom as Co-Investigator on a second AHRC large-grant project, *Creative Multilingualism*. She has published widely in the field of language education and is co-author of *Learning to Teach Foreign Languages in the Secondary School* (Routledge, 2014), *Language Development and Social Integration of Students with English as an Additional Language* (Cambridge University Press, 2020), and co-editor (with Wendy Ayres-Bennett) of *Multilingual Identity: Interdisciplinary Perspectives* (Cambridge University Press, forthcoming).

Karen Forbes is Associate Professor in Second Language Education at the Faculty of Education, University of Cambridge. She previously taught Modern Languages in a secondary school in England and has also taught English as a foreign language in Spain and China. Her current research interests include multilingual identity, the development and transfer of language learning strategies, and English as an Additional Language learners in schools. She is author of *Cross-linguistic Transfer of Writing Strategies: Interactions Between Foreign Language and First Language Classrooms* (Multilingual Matters, 2020) and co-author of *Language Development and Social Integration of Students with English as an Additional Language* (Cambridge University Press, 2020).

Christina Gkonou is Associate Professor of TESOL and MA TESOL Programme Leader in the Department of Language and Linguistics at the University of Essex, UK. She convenes postgraduate modules on teacher education and development, and on psychological aspects surrounding the foreign language learning and teaching experience. She is co-editor of *New Directions in Language Learning Psychology* (Springer, 2016), (with Sarah Mercer and Dietmar Tatzl); *New Insights into Language Anxiety: Theory, Research and Educational Implications* (2017), (with Jean-Marc Dewaele and Mark Daubney); and *The Emotional Rollercoaster of Language Teaching* (Multilingual Matters, 2020), (with Jean-Marc Dewaele and Jim King). She is also co-author of *MYE: Managing Your Emotions Questionnaire* (with Rebecca L. Oxford) and has published a number of research articles in international, peer-reviewed journals. Her new co-authored book (with Kate Brierton) is on *Cultivating Teacher Wellbeing* (Cambridge University Press, 2022).

Ben Knight works for Oxford University Press as Head of Language Content Research and Pedagogy. At the time of writing, he was the Director for Language Research for Cambridge University Press. His responsibilities included ensuring that high-quality research underpins the learning materials, curriculum development and teacher support that CUP provides. Ben has taught and worked in several countries around the world with International House, the British Council, Cambridge Assessment, City & Guilds, and various other schools and universities.

Judit Kormos is Professor in Second Language Acquisition in the Department of English Language and Linguistics at Lancaster University. She was a key partner in the award-winning DysTEFL project, sponsored by the European Commission, and is a lead educator in the Dyslexia and Foreign Language Teaching massive open online learning course offered by FutureLearn. She is co-author of the book *Teaching Languages to Students with Specific Learning Differences* (Multilingual Matters, 2021), (with Anne Margaret Smith). She has published widely on the effect of dyslexia on learning additional languages, including a book entitled *The Second Language Learning Processes of Students with Specific Learning Difficulties* (Routledge, 2017). She is the author of multiple research papers that investigate the role of cognitive factors in second language acquisition.

Betsy Parrish is Professor in the MA TESOL and TEFL Certificate programmes at Hamline University in St. Paul, Minnesota. She has worked as a language teacher, teacher educator and consultant for over 35 years, with experience in the US, Bangladesh, France, India, Russia and Vietnam. She has participated in the development of state and national adult education standards, focusing on college and career readiness. Her research centres around instruction that prepares English learners for success in today's world. Her most recent book, *Teaching Adult English Language Learners* (Cambridge University Press, 2019), addresses the diverse needs of adult English learners and provides ideas on how to prepare all learners for the demands of the twenty-first century.

Hayo Reinders is TESOL Professor at Anaheim University, California, and is Director of their doctoral programme. He is also Professor of Applied Linguistics at KMUTT in Thailand and editor of *Innovation in Language Learning and Teaching* (Springer, 2019). Hayo's interests are in CALL, autonomy, and out-of-class learning, topics that he explores at www.innovationinteaching.org. His most recent books are on teacher autonomy, teaching methodologies, and second language acquisition.

Silvana Richardson is Head of Education at Bell UK, Academic Director at Bell Teacher Academy, Cambridge, England, and Strategic Education Adviser at The Bell Foundation. She has worked in the field of English language teaching for 35 years as teacher, academic manager, teacher educator, inspector and consultant. She has trained EFL, MFL, ESOL, EAL, CLIL and subject teachers, teacher trainers and school leaders in the state and private sectors, both in the UK and abroad. She was Director of the Bell Delta Online, has written online materials for teachers, and is a speaker at international conferences. Silvana has co-written two Cambridge papers in ELT with Scott Thornbury and Gabriel Diaz Maggioli, and is the author of a forthcoming book on Professional Development for Cambridge University Press.

Graham Skerritt is studying for a PhD in Applied Linguistics and TESOL at the University of Leicester. He has taught in Japan for more than ten years and currently teaches part-time at two universities in Tokyo. He has also worked as a writer and editor of English language teaching materials for more than 15 years, including editing a number of titles for the methodology list at Cambridge University Press. His research interests include memory, vocabulary acquisition and blended learning.

Kate Wilson is an adjunct Associate Professor at the University of Canberra. She is a lecturer and researcher in TESOL, and was previously Head of the School of Languages and International Education, and Director of the Academic Skills Program at the University of Canberra. Her research interests include critical thinking and ELT, first year transition to university, and academic literacy.

Peter Watkins has been involved in teacher education for many years and currently works at the University of Portsmouth, UK. His main research interests relate to teacher education and teacher education materials writing. His publications include *Teaching and Developing Reading Skills* (Cambridge University Press, 2018); *Learning to Teach English* (Delta Publishing, 2nd edition 2014, 1st edition 2005); *Cambridge English Teacher: Vocabulary and Pronunciation* (Cambridge University Press, 2012) and *The CELTA Course Trainee Book* and *The CELTA Course Trainer's Manual* (both co-authored with Scott Thornbury, Cambridge University Press, 2007). He is also the author of the Cambridge White Papers 'Extensive reading in ELT: what and how?' (2018) and 'Extensive reading for primary in ELT' (2018).